# MARY MAGDALENE

## INSIGHTS FROM ANCIENT MAGDALA

Unveiling the Mystery with Perspectives
from Archaeology, Scriptures, and Historical Traditions

CW01500474

> ❝The story of Mary Magdalene reminds everyone of a fundamental truth: She is a disciple of Christ who, in the experience of human weakness, has had the humility to ask for his help, has been healed by him, and has followed him closely, becoming a witness of the power of his merciful love, which is stronger than sin and death.
>
> — Pope Benedict XVI, Angelus Address
> LES COMBES, JULY 23, 2006

Jennifer Ristine
Magdalena Institute
Magdala, Holy Land

MAGDALA TOURIST CENTER, LTD.
Migdal Junction
PO BOX 366
1495000 Migdal, Israel

Follow Magdala at:
www.magdala.org
www.facebook.com/ExperienceMagdala
@Magdala_Galilee

RCSpirituality Center

Follow RCSpirituality at:
www.rcspirituality.org
www.facebook.com/RCSpirituality

Cover design, drawings,and colored illustrations by Danielle Storey
Layout and design by Coronation Media

ISBN 978-107-766-019-9
First edition July 22, 2018

# MARY MAGDALENE

## INSIGHTS FROM ANCIENT MAGDALA

*Dedicated to my two VERY best friends—*

*You know who you are!*

"Readers will find a well-researched work that covers multiple aspects and theories posited about St. Mary Magdalene, from a picture of life in the Magdala of Mary's time uncovered by archaeology, through the various known, traditional, and theoretical narratives of her life and work, to the depiction of this powerful and enigmatic woman in art. Importantly, beyond fact and theory, the author gracefully creates the link between the experiences of Mary's life and the message of redemption she lived and proclaimed, and then translates this to the life of the reader, making this so much more than a scholarly look at Mary Magdalene but a work of hope quite relevant to today.

Maribeth Stewart
PRESIDENT, NATIONAL COUNCIL OF CATHOLIC WOMEN


"Every Christian disciple has so much to learn from the real Mary Magdalene. Jennifer Ristine helps sift fact from fiction, Gospel from pseudo-gospel, feminine genius from feminine gnosticism, in a way that will help everyone get to know, love, and imitate the once demon-dominated woman who became the great Apostle to the Apostles. This is a book to buy, read, and gift to friends and family.

Fr. Roger J. Landry
AUTHOR OF *PLAN OF LIFE: HABITS TO HELP YOU GROW CLOSER TO GOD*


"Through engaging deeply with ancient Jewish Magdala and with the rich legends surrounding this first century Jewish woman, Mary Magdalene, Jennifer Ristine has truly shown the fruitfulness of delving into the Jewish roots of Christianity. Magdala has all the possibility and responsibility to be a true site of Jewish-Christian encounter. This book is an important piece of that encounter.

Dr. Faydra L. Shapiro
EXECUTIVE DIRECTOR OF ISRAEL CENTER FOR JEWISH-CHRISTIAN RELATIONS

# TABLE OF CONTENTS

## NOTES OF GRATITUDE

Thank you to the many people who in some way are a part of this work. I thank those who opened my eyes to the wonders and mysteries of archaeology, especially those directly involved in the Magdala excavation and publications of material (Marcela Zapata, Arfan Najjar, Rosaura Sanz, Andrea Garza, Rina Talgam, Dina Avshalom-Gorni, Motti Aviam, and Luis Jurado).

To my community who supported the many hours of dedication required to publish a book from start to finish, for their feedback and patience through it all (Celine Kelly, Johanna Von Siemens, Christiane Esser, Mary Monette, Graciela Magaña, and Maria Ángeles Delgado). Fr. Eamon Kelly, LC, thank you for the constant bouncing of ideas, encouragement, and guidance. To my parents, Wayne and Mary Ristine, for their eyes and editorial skills. To Heather Luke for her patient and multiple run-throughs. Thank you to Danielle Storey for the gift of her artistic talent at the service of this project. And to so many others involved, including Fr. Fernando Tamayo, Fr Juan Solana, David Delgado, Felipe Arcile, Mariana Bravo, Hermana Viljoen, and the many Magdala staff and volunteers who had a hand in the project at some part of the journey in a practical way or through encouragement.

Above all, thanks to the Holy Spirit who first introduced me to Mary Magdalene and the message of Jesus' unconditional and personal love that she continues to preach today.

## AUTHOR'S NOTE

For the last four years, I have fielded questions about Mary Magdalene and Magdala's history and archaeology as I served in ancient Magdala, giving tours to countless visitors and offering interviews to the media. Tour guides have requested more information. I hope this work can serve you in some way. Visitors have asked for books on both Magdala and Mary Magdalene. I hope that this answers some of your questions. I am aware that multiple theories exist about her. While I subscribe to some and not to others, it is my hope that this work serves to value various approaches and ideas about her. It is always a challenge in our culture to maintain a mindset that is open and willing to learn, that seeks common ground amidst varied opinions, while remaining faithful to one's personal convictions.

Beyond factual research, I finally decided it was also time to put my personal insights onto paper. Do not expect that this book will answer all your questions about Mary Magdalene, because she remains a mystery, in a real and theological sense. A mystery, in its basic definition, is that which is unknown and secret. In theology, a mystery is an aspect of revelation that remains beyond our full comprehension, while at the same time we partly grasp it in faith. More than grasping a mystery with our intellect, we can enter into its dynamic. The mystery of Jesus' sacrificial death, for example, is beyond our human capacity to grasp in all its significance and greatness. Nonetheless, in our personal suffering or in prayer, we touch the mystery and unite ourselves to the suffering of Jesus, allowing it to bear fruit in our spiritual journey, as his suffering bore fruit for the redemption of humanity.

Mary Magdalene's person and life represent a mystery. Many details elude us. But the essential message of her life-project shines out for all to admire. She exemplifies the drama of redemption at work within every human person. She embodies the dynamics of the Christian life in its fullness, from sinner to seeker, from curious follower to committed disciple. Reflecting on the mystery of her person we find encouragement for our journey.

Despite the fact that the totality of her figure is "veiled," a glimpse into her person reveals essential universal messages with which all can identify: the deep need to experience unconditional love and acceptance, the desire to be set free of the toil and turmoil of life's demands, the joy of encountering the Lord, the fortitude experienced when God's grace and the Holy Spirit take over, and the hope that Jesus offers us throughout our lives.

I would like to "unveil" some of the mystery surrounding the person of Mary Magdalene by sharing insights gained through study, reflection, and prayer on the archaeology, geography, and history of ancient Magdala, as well as the scriptural passages and historical traditions prevalent through the centuries. I will also present the dynamic of her encounter with Jesus, hoping that it can serve as a reflection for your personal journey with the Lord.

# INTRODUCTION

I liken contemporary writings on Mary Magdalene to an ancient mosaic. Despite the wear and tear that disfigured the original image over the years, something remains of the essence and foundation. Art historians look at the ancient mosaic and offer their opinions about the original composition and design. Restorers piece it back together, giving it a renewed luster and beauty. In its newness, we see something of the original. The present day mosaic remains only an approximation of the real thing, yet with new insights and interpretations.

From the myriad tales that come to us today about Mary Magdalene, some are beautiful and edifying, some are aggravating and far-fetched, and some are curious or even astonishing. I often wonder if Mary Magdalene is looking down from heaven amused at us, wondering what on earth we will come up with next. Of one thing, I am certain. She would prefer that all conversation about her point the way to Jesus. As I expose insights into the world and person of Mary Magdalene, remember that she was a unique person, just like each of us. She grew up in a very specific culture and had particular personality traits that influenced her daily decisions. Life circumstances threw her some challenges. She may have faced them virtuously in some moments and failed in others. She was as human as the rest of us. This is her charm. In the messiness of life, Jesus met her where she was and offered her a new and better way. No matter where we are in our life, Jesus does the same for us. Every day his hand is outstretched to invite us forward, to begin a new day. Hope keeps us focused on the ultimate horizon.

That being said, the following information and reflections on Mary Magdalene are by no means dogmatic. Eager researching does not assure the discovery of truth even in historical matters. A number of contradictory claims about Mary Magdalene exist. History is interpreted. Nevertheless, it can offer us approximations of the reality. Does this make all things relative? There is no truth? Not in the least. It merely reinforces that authors interpret what they perceive from the evidence before their eyes. Worldviews, philosophical stances, or pastoral intentions can influence an author's perspective. This variance speaks of one essential truth: that we are searching for something real, something that sheds light on our ongoing life project. Mary Magdalene was real. Her life challenges, struggles, and joys were real. Her life was truly transformed by Jesus. It is possible to "unearth" pieces of what is real by digging through the layers of two thousand years of reflection about her. And in the process of discovery, we may glean treasures for our own life that inspire purpose and meaning.

View from Mount Arbel: Magdala at Sunrise.

# PART I: MARY MAGDALENE'S HOMETOWN

*Insights from Archaeology, History, & Geography*

---

Walking around the ruins of ancient Magdala conjures up the ambiance of Mary Magdalene's times. Archaeological discoveries and historical sources present Magdala as an economically thriving city in the time of Jesus. Most scholars claim that Magdala was one of the wealthier and larger cities on the western shore of the Sea of Galilee. Flavius Josephus referred to the city as Taricheae.[1] Visitors can imagine the cultural flavor of ancient Magdala thanks to evidence of a religious Jewish population, as well as the discoveries of Greco-Roman and Hellenistic remains. Through a brief survey of history and archaeology, aspects of Mary Magdalene's hometown begin to take shape. If the ancient stones and text may appear dry and boring, a Gospel imagination can give life to her town.

## HISTORICAL PANORAMA

### THIRD CENTURY BC TO PRESENT-DAY MIGDAL

Magdala began as a modest settlement around the third century BC. A greater city, however, was founded around the second century (c. 135 BC) at a time when John Hyrcanus annexed Judea and Galilee to expand the Hasmonean dynasty, leading to Jewish resettlement in the Galilee region. During the first century BC, Magdala politically aligned itself with the Jewish Hasmonean ruler and the Parthians against the Romans. Around 52 BC the Roman governor, Cassius, captured Magdala and according to Josephus, enslaved about thirty thousand Jews.[2] Despite this, Magdala recovered and flourished in the early Roman period under the rule of Herod the Great from 37 BC to 4 AD, and then of his son, Herod Antipas, until 39 AD.

In the time of Mary Magdalene, Magdala was already a thriving commercial fishing town and the capital of a toparchy in eastern Galilee. Its glory days came to an end with the Jewish Revolt and Roman conquest in 67 AD. The capture, killing, and enslaving of many of the inhabitants brought about a considerable change to the city.[3] Archaeologists believe that shortly after the conquest, flooding covered the northern side of Magdala, burying and thus preserving it for almost two thousand years. On the southern part of town, there is evidence of continued occupation, albeit of a smaller population, through the Byzantine, Crusader, and Ottoman periods.

The town maintained its tradition as the hometown of Mary Magdalene through the centuries. Christian pilgrims and travelers from the twelfth to the seventeenth centuries documented their discovery of a beautiful church, identified as the site of Mary Magdalene's house.[4] During the Ottoman period, a small Arab village was established over the ruins and preserved the name that commemorated the site. In 1935, the Franciscan Custos was tipped off about its significance by the last inhabitants of the Arab village of El-Mejdel ("the tower").[5] Archaeologists Sylvester Saller and Bellarmino Bagatti studied the visible archaeology on the site, making note of a spring near the tower, called "Sitti Myriam," in memory of Mary Magdalene. They also found the remains of an apse, a stone bearing a cross and the date 1389.[6] The site was destroyed in the 1948 Arab-Israeli conflict.

Modern-day Magdala was built by German Catholics and Russian Zionists from 1885 to 1910 on the hill to the northwest of the ancient ruins. The growing town continues today under the Hebrew name of *Migdal*, also meaning "tower." The name offers proof of continuity and identification with the traditionally celebrated hometown of Mary Magdalene. By 1970 the Franciscans became the custodians of a portion of the land holding Ancient Magdala, and the first excavations began. In 2009, the Legionaries of Christ, another religious congregation in the Catholic Church, purchased property next to the Franciscan site and discovered the northern part of the ancient town.

El Mejdel, 1910[7]

## MAGDALA'S INHABITANTS

Who were the Galileans of Magdala in Mary's time? Assuming that Magdala is indeed Taricheae, Flavius Josephus gives us a clue.[8]

> For as I know that this city of yours [Taricheae] was a city of great hospitality, and filled with an abundance of such men as having left their own countries, and are come hither to be partakers of your fortune, whatever it be, I had a mind to build walls about it,...[9]

Josephus refers to men who had left their countries. Were they Jews fleeing Judea to join the revolt? Were they Gentiles? Ancient Magdala appears to have been a predominantly Jewish town, possibly interspersed with Gentiles. Marcela Zapata, leading archaeologist and professor at Anahuac University, reports that the remains from the first-century BC suggest a predominantly Jewish occupation in the western side of the town. However, other cultural clues are evident in the eastern side of town. Close to the harbor, an industrial-like zone with a different architectural structure and very few Jewish remains suggest a Roman or Gentile presence from the first to the second century AD (up until the Bar Kobha Revolt, c. 135 AD).[10]

The question of Magdala's cultural assimilation or cultural juxtaposition remains. Was Magdala a Jewish city that absorbed the Hellenistic culture of its days? Was there a juxtaposition of cultures? Or were the Hellenistic influences merely a natural part of the historical development within city planning and architectural fashions? Historians and archaeologists continue to ponder the possibilities.[11]

## JEWISH VERSUS GRECO-ROMAN INFLUENCE

Excavations in the Galilee region generally reveal settlements of people with traditional Jewish beliefs and practices. Jewish ritual purification baths (mikva'ot), discus clay lamps with Jewish symbols, chalk stone vessels, ossuaries, and Hasmonean coins are prevalent. The absence of pagan shrines and non-kosher animal bones are notable. Considering the topography and location of the Galilee, however, the residents would not have been isolated from surrounding cultures. Magdala's excavations are a perfect example. Archeologist Stefano De Luca calls Magdala "a Jewish counterpart to other Hellenistic cities," such as those found in the Decapolis to the east or Hula Valley to the north.[12] Many parts of this excavation reveal Greek and Roman influences: Hellenistic-style urban planning, a Hasmonean Greek bathhouse and gymnasium, mosaics with Hellenistic-era designs, and frescoes with an early Roman period style.

Magdala's urban planning appears intentionally Hellenistic and in the style of a Hippodamian grid. It is a simple plan and widely used since the time of Alexander the Great. According to De Luca, these are the earliest examples of Hellenistic-style urban planning in Jewish Galilee.

Hippodamian grid (courtesy of Franciscan Biblicum)

In the early 1970s the Franciscans excavated a Hasmonean Greek bath house.[13] In 2015, Bauckham and De Luca made a new analysis of the excavations and gave their perspective on the importance of these findings.

> The baths are important as an instance of Hellenization and Romanization that goes beyond Greek language or Roman architecture in that it entails the adoption of a whole dimension of everyday life that had no precedent in traditional Jewish culture but was universal in the urban cultures of the Greco-Roman world. At the same time, it was adapted. (...) The baths of Magdala represent a more public acculturation of Jewish city culture to Hellenistic ways, for baths brought with them the culture of communal relaxation and recreational exercise for which they existed in the Hellenistic world. The Hasmoneans did not introduce them in Jerusalem, for example, where cultural conservatism might still have made them unwelcome, but in the new city they founded they were probably able to exercise a free hand.[14]

The artwork found in ancient Magdala shows the influence of the early Roman period, popular in the time of Herod the Great. For example, a meander-style mosaic decorates three different areas: (1) a bathhouse complex in the southern excavations, (2) the synagogue, and (3) a wealthy villa or complex in the northern excavations.[15] An eight-petalled rosette, which is a distinct and popular motif typical of the Herodian period, is found together with the meander design in both the synagogue and villa compound.[16]

Meander style mosaic in the Magdala synagogue

A wealthy villa mosaic, similar to the synagogue mosaic

Replica of the Greek bathhouse mosaic
(Originally found on the Franciscan excavated property)

The bathhouse-gymnasium houses a partially preserved first-century mosaic. The depictions include a first-century fishing boat, equipment used for exercising and bathing, an ancient Greek cup used to drink wine (*kantharos*), and a Greek inscription (ΚΑΙ ΣΥ), meaning "you too." The wording served to either drive away demons or welcome bathers, or both. Most surprising was a partial and rough representation of what seems to be a dolphin. The artwork in Magdala is faithful to the Jewish prohibition of images with the singular exception of this dolphin. A possible explanation is that this was a private area, in which case it might have been permissible. The dolphin image and the curious detail of two Roman dice found on a mosaic floor near the purification baths have provoked interesting speculation about the make-up of the town. It is difficult to ascertain if the dice reinforce the theory of the presence of non-Jewish residents or the dice were merely "left behind" by Roman troops after an invasion.

## CULTURAL CROSSROADS

Throughout the late Hellenistic and Roman periods, Galilean Jews interacted with their pagan neighbors, particularly those on the Mediterranean coast. Magdala's geographical location made it a prime spot for this crossroads of cultures through its large-scale commercial interactions. The city is nestled between the towering Mount Arbel and the shores of the Sea of Galilee. Historians speculate that part of the *Via Maris*, an ancient trade route, came through or nearby Magdala. The *Via Maris* linked Egypt, Syria, Anatolia, and Mesopotamia, offering paths for commerce and trade through the Jezreel and Jordan Valleys. Goods were imported and exported in all directions: by way of the Sea of Galilee directly east towards the Decapolis, north to Capernaum, by way of the *Via Maris* to Damascus, or across to the Mediterranean Sea and west to Rome. Mary Magdalene may have come into contact with those who frequented Magdala on their daily business.

An hour's walk to the south would bring Mary Magdalene to Galilee's capital, Tiberias, built by the Roman client king, Herod Antipas around 20 AD.[17] The controversial foundation over a cemetery discouraged Jews from settling there. Hence Herod Antipas sought non-Jews to populate his new capital. This new town would have increased the trading possibilities with Romans.[18]

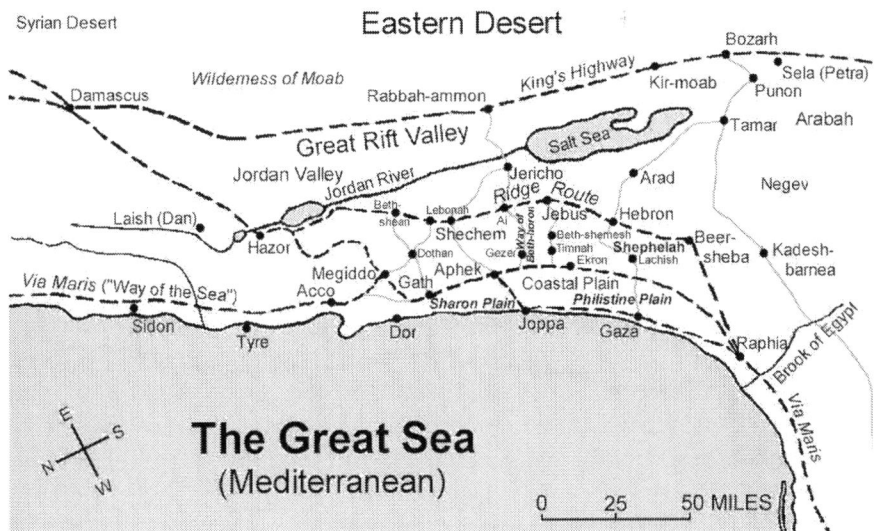

Highways in Ancient Times (Via Maris, King's highway)
(http://www.bibarch.com/images/Map-Regions.jpg)

Map of Israel (first-century)

According to the Christian tradition, Jesus frequently stayed in Capernaum during his public ministry (Mt 4:13). Capernaum is approximately ten kilometers (6 miles) northeast of Magdala, a two-hour walk along the shoreline of the Sea of Galilee. It is a comparatively short distance from Magdala compared to a two-day journey to Nazareth. As word of his healing power spread, large crowds began searching for him. People came from various places in Galilee, from the Decapolis, Jerusalem, Judea, Idumea, Tyre, Sidon, and from the region across the Jordan (Mt 4:25, Mk 3:8). The geographical area of these peoples extends from Syria in the north all the way south to the Dead Sea, and from the coast of the Mediterranean Sea to the pagan Decapolis on the eastern shore of the Sea of Galilee. Were they coming specifically to see Jesus? Or did they happen to be traveling on business and catch wind of this healer? Surely Mary Magdalene was abreast of the wonders being worked by Jesus near Magdala and crossed paths with the travelers coming from all parts.

## THE MARKETPLACE & FISH INDUSTRY

The economic success of Magdala involved, without a doubt, the fishing industry. The Jewish Talmud, a fourth-century AD source, referred to Magdala as *Migdal Nunya*, meaning "tower of fish." By 2009, archaeologists had uncovered a large round fish pool, thirteen meters in diameter, close to the seashore and a short distance from the ancient marketplace.

Excavated fish pool discovered in the northern area near the harbor[19]

The fish pool has been reconstructed in the guest house lobby on a slightly smaller scale

The marketplace contains about eight water shafts that look like a type of well or mikveh with a series of steps down to an unpaved bottom. They would have contained groundwater. Next to these are a series of smaller water installations. Until 2018 these were believed to be fish pools for displaying the fresh or salted fish on sale.[20] This theory is presently under debate. Nonetheless, Magdala has the reputation for being a great place for fish business.

Magdala's fame for its fish made it into the writings of Flavius, Strabo, Cicero, and Suetonius. This important export, valued by all social strata, provided lucrative income and sustenance for the residents. In addition to fresh fish, they may have been busy selling dried, salted, or pickled fish, as well as fish sauce (*garum*) or paste (*allec*). Preparing multiple fish products would allow the townspeople to make the most of each part of the fish. Marcela Zapata commented that to date Magdala lacks the archaeological evidence to indicate a salted fish processing area. The usual practice of fish processing took place at the harbor, well away from a synagogue, due to the smell. Hence the archaeological debate around the numerous water installations so close to the synagogue: were they created for commerce in the marketplace or for religious practice near the synagogue?

Excavating a well

Fish pools in industrial area (courtesy of IAA)

The excavated portion of the marketplace contains approximately 25 shops. The first-century Greek geographer and historian Strabo helps us imagine a bustling marketplace. "At the place called Taricheae the lake supplies excellent fish for pickling, and on its banks grow fruit-bearing trees resembling apple trees."[21] Talmudic sources help to paint a picture of the variety and scope, the color and sound in ancient Magdala's marketplace. A variety of goods are being sold, from preserved fish to woven wool to pigeons for Temple sacrifices, alongside luscious agricultural products harvested from the fertile land of Gennesaret.[22] Gennesaret was a tract of land four miles long on the western border of the Sea of Galilee, lying between current day Tabgha and ancient Magdala. Known as the "Paradise of Galilee," here farmers could grow and harvest walnuts, dates, olives, figs, and grapes.[23] Mary Magdalene would have watched the rich harvests of the land come and go through the marketplace.

Marketplace shops

Wash basin on the road between the marketplace and synagogue

A blockade to the marketplace road using the synagogue column stones
(Hypothesized to be part of the defense against the Roman invasion of 67 AD)

## THE HARBOR

The large fishing industry and bustling trade would have kept the harbor busy. Archaeologists have uncovered part of the ancient port. Ruins of a Hasmonean period watchtower at the harbor's edge stand on the southern, Franciscan excavated plot. This is one explanation for the origin of the town's name, *Migdal*, meaning tower. Further north, part of the harbor, most likely in use up until 67 AD, reveals a stone wall, possibly a breakwater. Thirty paces inland from the shoreline are the well-preserved remains of a stone road running parallel to the shore. Archaeologists believe that both a warehouse and an additional marketplace were situated adjacent to the harbor. A mooring stone was also discovered along the stone wall, indicating how and where boats docked in the first century.[24]

Mooring stone at port

Depiction of ancient Magdala's harbor marketplace based on the archaeological finds

## REMINISCING AT THE HARBOR

A Gospel scene comes to mind here. After the miracle of the multiplication of the seven loaves of bread, Jesus gets into a boat and comes to the region of Magadan (Mt 15:39). Mark 8:10 refers to the same incident with the name *Dalmanoutha*. The name and place are disputed, being either Magdala or a speculated, but as yet unidentified, area north of Magdala.

Nonetheless, these ruins of the harbor and sea-side road offer Christians a composition of place for the possible comings and goings of Jesus and his disciples from the shores of Magdala. A contemporary worship center, Duc In Altum, was built in 2014 to commemorate the public life of Jesus and honor the dignity of women. The main altar abstractly replicates a first-century fishing boat as it floats above the ancient harbor. It is a place to imagine a curious Mary Magdalene keeping her eye on the charismatic and itinerant rabbi, Jesus of Nazareth. Perhaps she sat on the shoreline as he preached from the boat about the seed that falls on rocky, thorny, or fertile soil. Eventually, his word fell upon her soul like a seed in fertile soil (Mt 13:23).

Duc In Altum boat altar, built over the first-century harbor

# A WELL-TO-DO MAGDALA: VILLAS AND MIKVA'OT

In Mary Magdalene's day, Magdala was likely one of the wealthier cities on the western shores of the Sea of Galilee. Excavations have uncovered evidence of higher social strata. For example, two large living quarters lie south of the marketplace. They house several rooms of basalt-slabbed floors, in contrast to the more common and simpler dirt packed floor. One of the complexes contains a mosaic floor similar to the one found in the synagogue. Two Roman dice were discovered in this area. Each complex also contains two purification baths of excellent quality.

The ritual purification baths are known in Hebrew as *mikveh*, singular, or *mikva'ot*, plural. All four of the very well-preserved mikva'ot date from the late Second Temple period (1st century BC to 1st century AD). The baths attach to sitting rooms, one of which has the mosaic floor. Fallen-down archways boast of entrances that welcomed people to these fine quarters. It is uncertain if these two complexes were privy to individual families or to a network of families. The Talmud refers to a priestly family having its seat in Magdala. If that were the case in the first centuries BC and AD, the indoor mikva'ot would serve a lifestyle calling for a higher demand of ritual purity.

Aerial view of the mikva'ot area with mosaic sitting room

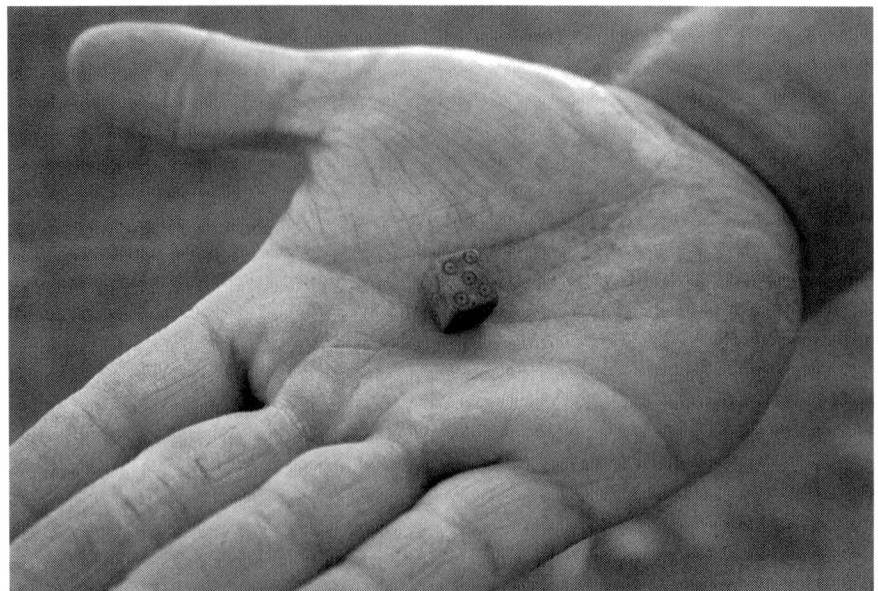

Roman dice

Discoveries of purification baths close to the Sea of Galilee cause historians and archaeologists to ponder their significance. It is most likely that the common people used the Sea for their purification purposes, while the wealthy enjoyed the relative comfort of indoor mikva'ot. They could also indicate the importance of upholding Jewish identity and customs to maintain the law of ritual purity. The two-meter-deep pools afforded privacy and represent the highest quality of ritual baths in the Jewish tradition.[25] Full immersion and nudity were required. They were used more frequently in the rainy, wintry season when the groundwater level was higher. First-century engineers would be proud of their legacy as, almost two thousand years later, water began flowing again as soon as excavators removed the dirt. They continue to function to the present day.

Professor Marcela Zapata oversaw this excavation. She commented:

❝These mikva'ot are unique in Israel due to the subterraneous water that flows through them. This makes them the purest type in conformity with the Mishnah. The architectural design that connects the four different mikva'ot allows for the constant movement of living water, maintaining the quality for ritual purity.[26]

Mikveh, April 2018

Although both men and women used these baths, the law stipulates many more reasons for women to purify themselves than men. Menstruation, childbirth, and sexual intercourse render women ritually impure (Lev 11-15, 18:29). Even today, religious women need to immerse themselves in a mikveh before resuming marital relations. While blood signifies life (Lev 17:11), menstruation is part of the fertility cycle linked to death as it represents life unfulfilled. Childbirth also involves blood, and while there is some mystery as to why it renders the woman impure, Leviticus 12 refers to a stipulated time needed for purification. After a prescribed period, the women would complete the process with a mikveh. As a Jewish woman, Mary Magdalene would undoubtedly have been accustomed to this ritual.

A cistern with an intact archway

## JEWISH HERITAGE AND A CROSSROADS OF JEWISH AND CHRISTIAN HISTORY

### THE SYNAGOGUE

The most outstanding archaeological discoveries of the 2009 excavation were the synagogue and, within it, a Temple-model stone. The synagogue was found just one meter below the surface. Dina Avshalom-Gorni and Arfan Najjar of the Israeli Antiquities Authorities reported that the building was over an earlier Hasmonean-period foundation.[27] Several coins found inside the synagogue help to date its use within the first century AD. The oldest identifiable coin, found at the level of the synagogue foundation, dated to around 5 AD and was minted by one of Augustus' Roman governors. The discovery of a 29 AD coin, minted in the reign of Herod Antipas, confirms the belief that the synagogue was in use during the public life of Jesus. Another coin, minted in 43 AD and found on top of the mosaic floor, feeds the hypothesis that synagogue renovations were undertaken at this later date.

Aerial view of the synagogue

Coin found in the synagogue
(minted in 29 AD)

Roman coin 5-11 AD
similar to the one found in the synagogue

Frescoes in the synagogue, early Roman period

Fresco remnants hint at a once-beautifully decorated space with six columns and walls all painted with intensely colorful pigments. The style resembles early Roman period frescoes in Pompeii. Basalt stone benches line the once-beautifully frescoed walls. Another square of benches towards the center of the room allows people to sit even closer to the middle of the synagogue, where the readers and rabbis would stand for ceremonial moments. Archaeologists identify a small mosaic-floored room in the corner of the synagogue as the *Aron HaKodesh*, the place where the religious leaders stored the Torah and other scrolls.

Many scholars hold the opinion that the first-century synagogue was not a place of worship, but a type of community center or assembly hall (*Bet-Knesset* in Hebrew).[28] In addition to standard administrations of law, such as punishment for not paying taxes, the synagogue was the central place for Torah reading, studying, discussion, and teaching. We see Jesus keeping this practice as it was his custom to visit the synagogue on the Sabbath (Lk 4:16, Mk 1:21, Mk 6:2, Lk 13:10, Lk 6:6). It is highly likely that Jesus taught in the synagogue of Magdala, because of Magdala's prominence, location, and the witness of the Gospel of Matthew: "Jesus went throughout Galilee, teaching in their synagogues, proclaiming the Good News of the kingdom, and healing every disease and sickness among the people" (Mt 4:23).

Torah storeroom (Aron HaKodesh)

When Jesus spoke in the synagogue at Nazareth, all eyes were fixed on him (Luke 4:20). His captivating presence would have attracted men and women alike. Would a woman, like Mary Magdalene, have been allowed to enter the synagogue in Jesus' time? Some argue yes. The Babylonian Talmud states, "A woman puts her food pots upon the stone, leaving her non-Jewish servant at home until she comes from the bathhouse or the synagogue."[29] While this source is from writings of the third to fifth century AD, it reflects traditionally held norms. Another Talmudic tract states, "All are qualified to be among the seven [who read publicly from the Torah in the synagogue on the Sabbath], even a minor or a woman."[30]

The synagogue stands witness to a Jewish presence in Magdala. Nonetheless, the question arises: Did any of the Jewish residents in Magdala begin to believe in Jesus as the Messiah? Certainly, they would know about Jesus' preaching and healings, and they would have heard news of his crucifixion and mysterious disappearance. Undoubtedly there were sincere followers throughout the region. The synagogue was likely in use up until the Revolt of 67 AD, during the after-effects of Jesus' resurrection and the beginning of the early Church. Standing around the ruins today, visitors can imagine the religious leaders receiving the news of Jesus' crucifixion and death. Word probably reached them that Mary Magdalene was spreading the "rumor" that Jesus was alive and that he had risen from the dead.

What is difficult to ascertain is whether the seeds of faith in Jesus as the Messiah were sown inside that synagogue. History may never be able to confirm this one way or the other, but the fact is that during the first three years of the site's official opening, over 360,000 visitors have stood around the ancient synagogue. Approximately 20 percent of those visitors have been local Israelis marveling at the uncovering of their Jewish heritage. Jewish visitors see the stones' testimony of a people linked so intricately to their past. The other 80 percent are Christians from over 100 countries.[31] Present-day Magdala offers a walk through a crossroads of Jewish and Christian history. The presence of Christians here today testifies to the living echo of Mary Magdalene's proclamation, "I have seen the Lord!" (John 20:18). Since that time, centuries of witnesses have followed the prompting of this woman whose testimony of faith continues to animate those who are called to spread the Good News.

## MAGDALA STONE

No archaeological find in Magdala broadcasts the Jewish heritage more than the Magdala Stone. It was providentially stumbled upon in the salvage excavation of the area planned for the new guesthouse's ecumenical chapel. It stands almost in the center of the synagogue. Archaeologists believe that the stone is a later addition to the synagogue, perhaps between the 40s and 50s. Its uniqueness has spurred much speculation about its use and significance. It has fostered debates that are likely to continue for several years.

Synagogue with the Magdala Stone

One of the debates involves the mode of interpretation. Steven Fine, historian of Judaism in the Greco-Roman era, challenged previous scholars with his object-centered approach. In a 2017 article, he wrote, "I see an object with imagery that is well known from first-century Judaea, particularly from architecture and funerary art and likely from furniture decoration."[32] His object-centered interpretation deconstructs previous religious interpretations of the symbols. He looks at the objects at hand without placing them within a pre-conceived religious narrative. For example, whereas previous scholars interpret two rosettes as Ezekiel's chariot (Ezek 1), Fine suggests that they can be mere space fillers that were a common art form of the time. Rosettes were one type of Roman art that was adopted by the Jews. Those found on the Magdala Stone are typical of others found throughout Judaea. In a world that thrives on secret meanings, Fine's more "mundane" approach, as he calls it, doesn't quite get the level of media attention accorded to the more religious and theological interpretations of his colleagues.

The other mode of interpretation is a holistic approach. Several scholars have compared the symbols on the Magdala Stone with objects found in the Jerusalem Temple. For this reason, it received the title of a "Temple model" stone. In 2013, Mordechai Aviam, archaeologist and professor of history, proposed that it acted as the base for a reading table.[33] A four-columned table stood on this stone to allow a person to read the Torah standing. Rina Talgam of the Hebrew University, whilst subscribing to the "Temple-model" theory, discarded the idea that the stone acted only as a base. She believes that the Magdala Stone was a type of "liturgical furniture" upon which the Torah rests directly.[34] She also stressed that the "Temple model" stood on display in the synagogue at the same time that the Second Temple was standing in Jerusalem, indicating the centrality of the Temple in the lives of ancient Magdala's residents. By 2015, Richard Bauckham said that "the stone symbolizes a cultic connection between the synagogue and the Temple."[35]

Front of Magdala stone (The stone contains the oldest carved menorah found in a public setting)

The depiction on Titus' arch in Rome shows the Roman soldiers carrying the Menorah out of the Temple. Titus' arch was constructed in 82 AD, twelve years after the Temple destruction[36]

A Menorah was carved into a wall in the priests' mansion of the Herodian quarter, prior to the Temple destruction in 70 AD.

The symbols are schematically carved into the solid limestone block, representing the main areas of the Temple. On one side, the seven-branch candelabra, called a Menorah, amazes experts. Art historians and archaeologists believe that the tripod base indicates the original artist's first-hand knowledge of the objects in the Temple. This Menorah may, in fact, be a more faithful rendition than the one carved on Titus' arch in Rome. The tripod base also resembles one found on the wall of a priestly mansion excavated in the Old City of Jerusalem near the Temple, giving further affirmation of the authentic depiction of the Menorah on the Magdala Stone.[37]

The top of the Magdala Stone contains symbols of showbread tables and a rosette. The rosette consists of six petals forming a flower with six petals encircling it. It is very similar to a mosaic floor design in the priestly mansion near the Temple. Rina Talgam interprets the rosette as a symbol of the veil dividing the Temple's sanctuary from the most sacred part of the Temple, the Holy of Holies.

If the stone is intended to be read symbolically as a model of the Temple, then one side of the stone represents the Holy of Holies, depicted with two wheels and triangles that resemble flames of fire. A reading of Ezekiel 1 and 10 or Daniel 7 conjures up the image of a fiery chariot as God's throne. With this reading, the symbol appropriately alludes to the *Shekinah*, God's glory that dwelt within the Holy of Holies.

A Rosette mosaic found inside the Priests' mansion
(Herodian Quarter), currently in Wohl Museum

Top of the Magdala Stone

Back of the Magdala Stone depicting fiery chariot wheels and interpreted
as an image for the Holy of Holies in the Second Temple

The rosette in Capernaum

Rosettes on archaeology discovered in Capernaum are similar to the rosettes on the back side of the Magdala Stone, possibly representing the Holy of Holies in the Second Temple

Rina Talgam offers a thought-provoking theory regarding the significance of the Magdala Stone for the first-century Jewish residents of Galilee. She comments:

❝The stone ... shows us that the communities in Galilee at that time had sentiments towards the Temple in Jerusalem, but on the other hand, something new began to emerge. This new thing is very important.

...The Temple model stood in the center, and the community stood around, surrounding the stone. The community, in a certain respect, replaced the Courts in the Temple of Jerusalem. And the community (itself) became a kind of Temple. The Temple is not just a building, but the community that practiced certain rituals.

In the Temple, only priests were allowed to enter and see those sacred vessels. Here [on the Magdala Stone] they [the sacred vessels] are displayed for the entire community. Each person can read the Torah; each person can preach in the synagogue.[38]

Rina believes that the stone points to new approaches in the history of religion, reflecting a crossroad of Jewish and Christian concepts, namely, the centrality of community worship and the role that each person plays within a spiritual practice. She believes it alludes to the emergence of a new way of worshipping God that did not rely solely on the Temple. If this were truly the case, it reconstructs an image of Magdala that corresponds to comments from Flavius Josephus and Tacitus, Jewish and Roman historians respectively. They reported that the time leading up to the destruction of the Temple (70 AD) was a time of mysterious premonition. Jesus, furthermore, predicted the destruction of the Temple (Mt 24: 1–2). The idea of a transition away from the centrality of worship in the Temple was in the air.[39] Is the Magdala Stone indicative of this transition within the Second Temple period? This question remains for further discussion among scholars.

## MAGDALA'S REPUTATION

Wealth, Jewish observance and religiosity, and Greco-Roman influence all weave together as we form an image of first-century Magdala. But the complexity of the town is compounded when we discover its historical reputation. A Jewish text, called the Lamentations Rabbati, refers to three wealthy towns destroyed for their sinfulness, one of which was Magdala.[40]

This Jewish text compiles the writings of sages up until the fourth century AD. If it is indeed referring to the hometown of Mary Magdalene, this would show its immoral reputation among the Jewish rabbis.

> *There were three cities whose taxes were carried to Jerusalem in wagons because of their great weight. The names of these three cities were Kabul [south east of Akko], Shihun [near Sepphoris], and Magdala [near Tiberias]. Why was Kabul destroyed? Because of their discords. Why was Shihun destroyed? Because of their magic arts. *Why was Magdala destroyed? Because of their harlotries.* [emphasis added]

If harlotries refer to prostitution, it was illegal in the Jewish culture, whereas in the Roman and Greek culture it was an accepted and institutional part of society. In both cultures, prostitutes were generally of the lowest social class. Except for beautiful courtesans of wealthy patrons, they were either slaves or freed women incapable of supporting themselves by any other means.[41] With the discovery of a wealthy town and the scriptural reference of Mary Magdalene supporting Jesus with her resources, her persistent reputation as a prostitute would therefore be highly questionable. She was most likely not a poor prostitute on the street, as popular culture often portrays her. But it appears that she does come from a town that was scandalous in the eyes of others. Perhaps the town's reputation has cast a shadow on Mary Magdalene across the centuries.

Uncertainty remains around the actual nature of the town, as well as the truth of Mary's reputation. Thomas McDaniel, a Hebrew studies scholar, proposes a different reputation than prostitution. He says that the word "harlotries" has a similar meaning to its Arabic cognate, *zûn*, meaning "an idol," leading him to propose that idolatry may have been more of a problem than prostitution. The first-century mosaic discovered in the Greek bathhouse offers a connection to this possibility. The image that De Luca and Bauckham have interpreted as a dolphin could have bordered on idolatry in the Jewish culture of the time. Scholars have long held the theory that animate objects in art were considered graven images in Jewish culture. They may have been perceived to be contrary to the second commandment. The earliest known use of animate figures in Jewish art is from 244 AD, the Dura-Europos synagogue (present-day Syria). Whether or not the image was perceived as idolatrous by the town's people themselves, it points to a cultural assimilation or mix of cultures that could have given Magdala a bad name in early Jewish history.

Associating Mary Magdalene with Magdala's reputation of idolatry, and looking at it from a Jewish perspective, could Mary's faithful devotion to the one person, Jesus, be construed as idol worship? As she followed him around Galilee, she may have gained a scandalous reputation among the townspeople. They may not have seen her inner world, a deeper conversion taking place, but only noticed her bold and independent character now completely channeled towards following a "miracle worker" and "crazy itinerant rabbi." It is possible that these strings of inferences are completely off target. Connecting the dots, however, brings about curious and inevitable ponderings. And the ancient ruins of Magdala are the perfect place to do just that.

## THE "DEATH AND RESURRECTION" OF MAGDALA

What happened to Magdala after Jesus' death and resurrection? From that time until the Jewish Revolt of 67 AD, neither historical texts nor archaeological discoveries offers us any evidence of the possible religious inclination of Magdala's residents towards Jesus as the Messiah. Literary sources, however, give clues to the political leaning during Flavius Josephus's military command. Despite initial intentions to avoid rebellion against Roman rule, zealous Jewish rebels ran into Magdala to take cover. Unfortunately for the residents, Roman troops came after them, invading Magdala.

### THE DEMISE OF MAGDALA

The "demise" of Magdala occurred around 67 AD, before the death of Nero and on the cusp of Vespasian's reign as Emperor. According to Flavius Josephus, Vespasian himself had a hand in this deadly blow. The number of people killed in and around Magdala far exceeds the city's estimated population of 4,000. The majority of those killed were likely rebellious zealots who rallied together for the Revolt against the Romans. Whilst the city of Magdala appears to have continued to function after this battle, it suffered a severe blow and population decline. Flavius's description leaves the impression that it was the most barbarous action undertaken by Vespasian during the Jewish Revolt and that the town slaughter and battle on the sea killed as many as 6,500 people. Survivors were escorted to Tiberias where a brutal fate awaited them. One thousand two hundred were deemed useless for labor and massacred. Six thousand young men were chosen as Nero's slaves to dig an Isthmus. Thirty thousand four hundred were sold as slaves, and the remaining were given as slave gifts to Agrippa.[42] Vespasian's son, Titus, would go on to conquer Jerusalem and destroy the Temple in 70 AD.

Roman invasion of 67 AD

## A WITNESS OF DEATH AND RESURRECTION

Near the beginning of Christianity, a great contrast is set up in history. On the one side, Vespasian, portrayed as a type of Messiah by historians such as Dio Cassius (Roman History Vol. 8, Book 65.8), stakes his claim as the Roman Emperor, and gains his position through horrendous violence. On the other side, for Christians, Jesus Christ, the true Messiah, suffered brutal torture at the hands of Roman rule, so winning a Kingdom for all through his self-sacrifice.

Before those two contrasts, the image of *Mary of Magdala* standing at the foot of the cross comes into focus. Destruction and death in her hometown, in her country, and of her beloved Jesus cause a torrent of tears and sufferings. Nonetheless, she also stands at the tomb as the first witness of the resurrection. She is there to say, "Death is not the end." In the face of horrendous tragedy, she bears the Good News that Jesus' victory still triumphs even through the dark valley of death. Christians still today need this message as persecution continues in places very near to Magdala.[43]

## MAGDALA: BEARING A TIMELESS MESSAGE

As early as the 1970s the Franciscan Fathers Virgilio Corbo and Stanislao Loffreda excavated part of the city of Magdala.[44] Excavations on this property continued from 2006 to 2012 by Stefano De Luca. In 2006, a Legionary of

Bar Mitzvah in the ancient synagogue, May 2018

Christ, Father Juan Solana, initiated labors to construct a guest house on the adjoining property, to the north of the Franciscan-owned Magdala. By 2009 the northern part of ancient Magdala, with the synagogue ruins, was discovered. As the custodians of this part of the ancient city of Mary Magdalene, the Legionaries of Christ, in conjunction with Anahuac University, continue to excavate. They anticipate other discoveries in years to come.

The "resurrecting" of the ancient town brings Mary Magdalene's voice to the forefront once again. She is "resurrected" in the twenty-first century, not as a lone heroine, but as a woman who points the way to the One who has the answer to our perennial human condition. The ancient ruins testify to her life. It was a life searching for hope, discovering it, and offering it to others as a witness to Jesus' redeeming love.

She reminds us that Jesus most likely walked through this town. He taught the multitudes, and he spoke personally to those who sought him out. He healed their brokenness. Some, like Mary Magdalene, followed him to Jerusalem, to his fate at the cross. Today, he invites everyone to do the same: to embrace the imperfections and challenges of daily life and to hope beyond the deplorable injustices that continue to plague a wounded humanity. It is a call to remain steadfast in our proclamation of the Good News and its promise for a restored humanity.

Mary Magdalene column in the Duc in Altum

# PART II: THE LIFE DRAMA OF MARY MAGDALENE

*Insights from Sacred Scriptures*

---

The Canonical Gospels are neither straight history nor biographies, but the testimony of faith based on historical events. They were written approximately 30 to 60 years after the actual events and were based on first-hand witness and oral tradition. They are inspired texts offering a universal message of salvation. Hence, what may be missing, such as names of characters and more explicit descriptions of personal experiences with Jesus, was not deemed essential for the early Christian community. This is where interpretations begin to abound on details of the life and person of Mary Magdalene. But the Canonical Gospels act as a foundational springboard for identifying prominent aspects of her life and her significance within the drama of history. We begin with the mere mention of her name.

## MARY OF MAGDALA OR MARY CALLED THE MAGDALENE?

The name, "Mary Magdalene," is present eleven times in the Gospels.[45] Some authors claim that the original scriptural text signifies Mary *of* Magdala. They conclude that she derives her name from the town, rather than from her father or spouse, as was common for women in the first century. If her name refers to the town, it indicates her independence and likely inheritance from her father or husband. Many conclude that she was a widow of influence. It may also imply that she spent a considerable amount of time in Magdala and that she owned a considerable amount of property in the town. A further conclusion is that Mary was at least of middle age when she encountered Jesus, having already established herself as an independent and wealthy woman.

Luke is the only evangelist who uses the expression "called the Magdalene" (Lk 8:2). The Greek word *kaloumenē* (καλουμένη) signifies "called," giving the impression that *Magdalene* is a sort of "nickname" or identifier of her character, more than referring to her town of origin. Benefactors of the early Church received new names, and so once she received the title "Magdalene," it would distinguish her from other women named Mary. The distinction would be necessary even if she were not a benefactor. In the Herodian period, the name Mary, with its multiple variations, was the second most popular female name.[46] Inscriptions on first-century AD ossuaries reveal this. From her nickname as Magdalene, she acquires diverse titles.[47]

Mary acquires the nickname *Tower of Strength*, which comes from the name of the town (*migdal* meaning tower) and its Hebrew cognate (*gadel* meaning great or strong). From the name *Mariam*, she becomes an *Ocean of Wisdom* (*Mar* meaning "master" or "learned person" and *Yam* meaning "sea" or "ocean"). This title fits the characteristics of the Mary Magdalene illustrated in the Gnostic gospels of the second to fifth centuries, due to the allusion that her wisdom far exceeded the disciples' understanding of Jesus' teachings.

When Magdalene is associated with the masculine plural noun גדלים (*gedilim*), meaning twisted threads, the association of her being a prostitute begins to take shape. Her association with the "*Miriam Megaddlela*" in a Jewish Talmudic tale, gives her the title of "Mary with the braided locks," making her a hairdresser. In the Jewish community, this title was equivalent to a woman in a non-reputable occupation, namely an adulteress or prostitute. Add to that the Greek translation *magdaliá*, meaning "dirt washed off," and the Mary Magdalene with a soiled reputation takes form.

By the sixth century, Pope Gregory the Great's conflation of Mary of Magdala with Mary of Bethany (John 12:1-8) and the sinful woman who anoints Jesus' feet (Luke 7:36-38) reinforced her reputation in Christian theology as a woman of ill repute.

From the mere mention and analysis of her name, she already acquired several personality traits and a reputation among other women. Is it possible that the disciples gave her the nickname, offering a multi-layered meaning to her title: she is both from Magdala and, besides being a substantial benefactor, she exhibits a sort of "towering" personality, bold and independent? As we read further, we see another reason she stands out from the crowd: her seven demons.

## MARY MAGDALENE, OUT OF WHOM
## HE HAD DRIVEN SEVEN DEMONS

*MARK 16:9; LUKE 8:2*

Both Mark and Luke remark that Mary Magdalene was a woman from whom seven demons were cast out. Among popular culture and scripture scholars, a plethora of interpretations exist. Ultimately, she undergoes some form of liberation and deep healing, be it physical, emotional, psychological, spiritual, or a combination of factors. The evangelists leave us to ponder the cause of her seven demons. They may reflect a life choice or a circumstance that was out of her control. Seven, a number referring to fullness, gives the sense of a very grave need to be set free from whatever afflicts her.

Writings throughout the centuries have predominantly associated her demons with a spiritual manifestation related to a pattern of life choices. The sixth-century Roman Catholic Pope Gregory the Great assumed that the seven demons were the result of a sinful life. He identified the seven demons with seven vices that Mary eventually overcomes, living virtuously. A seventh-century Greek Orthodox Patriarch, Modestus of Jerusalem, referred to the expulsion as a casting out of the prince of evil from human nature. The Greek tradition also reflects on her spiritual battle against passions. The twelfth-century writer, Theophanus Kerameus wrote:

> Let no one think that Mary had seven demons. But it is just as the gifts of the Holy Spirit are synonymously called seven spirits, as the great Isaiah numbered them (Is 11:2-3). Thus the energies of the demons are also called demons. Despondency, thriftiness, contempt, envy, falsehood, greed, and every passion is synonymous with the demon that begat it. Whoever is dominated by these passions is possessed by demons. Therefore it was not at all unlikely and impossible for Mary Magdalene to be possessed by seven passions, from which she was redeemed and became a disciple of the Savior.[48]

On the other hand contemporary authors, such as Dr. TJ Wray, often label the demons as signs of a mental or physical disorder, from a type of schizophrenia to epilepsy. In her book, *Good Girls, Bad Girls of the New Testament*, Dr. Wray states,

> The "seven demons" Jesus casts out of her most likely refer to a seizure disorder, like epilepsy, or any number of mental illnesses, such as schizophrenia. People during Jesus' day have little or no understanding of the etiology of neurological or mental disorders, instead attributing such maladies to demonic possession. It is likely, then, that Mary suffers from one of these disorders and that Jesus heals her.[49]

Throughout history, mental illness has been equated with demonic influences, many times falsely. Physical or mental illnesses, however, have been known to have deeper spiritual influences. In Luke 13:11 there is mention of a woman who is crippled *by a spirit* for eighteen years. While illnesses and demonic influences can be confused or related, Jesus himself makes a distinction between the two.

When Pharisees warn him that Herod wants to kill him, Jesus responds, "Go tell that fox, 'I will keep on driving out demons and healing people today and tomorrow, and on the third day, I will reach my goal'" (Luke 13:32). Jesus also gave instructions to the apostles to heal the sick and drive out demons, mentioning these two acts specifically (Mt 10:8).

The possibility of real possession or demonic influence on Mary Magdalene should not be altogether discredited. Contemporary scripture scholars Joseph Fitzmyer, John Nolland, and Francois Bovon all concur that the number of demons implies the severity of her state and suppose that Jesus performed an exorcism on her.[50]

Whatever the case of Mary Magdalene, surely Jesus was able to look upon her and know the truth of her situation and the extent of her need for liberation in whatever realm. Jesus came ultimately to heal the whole person and any healing he offers, be it physical, psychological, or spiritual, is by virtue of bringing each person to the ultimate healing: salvation.

Within this context, the ministry of Jesus involves a clash between the Kingdom of God and the kingdom of Satan. The numerous Gospel stories of Jesus expelling demons give the impression that Galilee is a spiritual "battleground." Mary Magdalene becomes one "arena" where this was played out. Jesus expels her seven demons, winning the victory against the afflictions plaguing her whole person.

Despite the triumph, Mary doesn't have it easy afterward. While Jesus ultimately won the victory of redemption, he applies that reward to those who enter into the mystery of his own life: his passion, death, and resurrection. Christians are called to enter into the dynamic of the Paschal mystery. Part of that dynamic necessitates a daily struggle, for the common strategy of the devil is to offer temptations.

Mary Magdalene, like the rest of humanity, certainly had to fight a life-long spiritual battle. St Paul testifies to this battle in general: "for our wrestling is not against flesh and blood; but against principalities and powers, against the rulers of the world of this darkness, against the spirits of wickedness in the high places" (Ephesians 6:12).

In our present culture, acceptance of sin, pornographic or substance addictions, idol worship, and occult practices have been known to open the door to demonic activity.[51] Possessions and oppressions are considered to be more serious demonic influences. Both disturb the normal functions of the person.

A possessed person can manifest facial distortions, rejections of anything holy, verbal vulgarities, and physical movements that could have the appearance of an epileptic attack. Those with oppressions can experience effects on their mental state, or experience chronic physiological or psychological pain such as a deep depression. This type of demonic influence can manifest itself in persons with addictive behaviors. While not all addictive behavior or depression equals possession, demonic spirits can seek to bind the person in their addictive state.[52]

Victims of unconsented traumas and violations against their dignity, such as sexual abuse, can also be provoked and assaulted by evil spirits. The wounds fester and fail to heal, perpetuating violence to self or to others. Once again, psychological elements can play a part, but spiritual assaults in the form of temptations may gain ground in a person's persistent anger or resentment and desire to seek revenge or to refuse forgiveness. Orna Grinman, a sexual abuse survivor and author of Who Is Knocking on Your Door, testifies that she experienced these temptations and the resulting torment in her conscience until she truly came to forgive her perpetrator.

Nonetheless, Jesus can heal and liberate us from the wounds of sexual assault or induced traumas. Denisse Bossert, freelance journalist and originator of Healing Dinah's Wound, comments on who Mary Magdalene has been for her, in the light of sexual trauma. She wrote, "The One who is Love sets Mary free from the wounds of exploitation and abuse, Himself filling up the space left behind when darkness is expelled. I see the woman from Magdala as a sign that when Christ sets us free, we are truly free."[53]

Acknowledging the real influence of evil spirits has led to reflections on what the Gospel writers depict as Mary Magdalene's need for liberation from the effects of demonic influence. It neither makes her a victim nor defames her by labeling her as a sinner. It simply reinforces the fact that she is human. And more powerfully, it reveals the beauty of redemptive love at work within her life. Her "being set free of seven demons" speaks of realism, liberation, and hope. From her experience of liberation, she becomes a faithful follower and supporter of Jesus.

# THE WOMEN ACCOMPANIED AND CARED FOR JESUS

## *MARK 15:4; LUKE 8:1-3*

Luke states that "The Twelve were with him, and also some women who had been cured of evil spirits and diseases: Mary (called Magdalene) from whom seven demons had come out; Joanna the wife of Chuza, the manager of Herod's household; Susanna; and many others. These women were helping to support them out of their own means" (Lk 8:1-3). Luke's comment leads scholars to propose that Mary was a wealthy woman. The only evangelist who puts her at the end of a list of women is John. John lists Jesus' blood relatives first, starting with his mother, then his aunt Mary Cleopas, and finally Mary Magdalene. Since she is listed first by the other evangelists, she most likely had a more prominent role or "higher status" than the others.

Mary Magdalene was not the only prominent woman accompanying and supporting Jesus. Luke groups her with another woman who was possibly involved in Herod's court. Johanna was the wife of Chuza, Herod's steward or administrator. Inferring a relationship between these women contradicts the popular belief that Mary Magdalene was a poor street prostitute. Raymond Bruckberger makes this connection in his book, *Maria Magdalena*. He proposes that at a young age, Mary Magdalene fed her mind with romanticized readings of biblical stories such as Judith and Esther, or the ancient Greek courtesan, Phryne. Her desires to use her alluring beauty led her to court life, introducing her to the licentious and pagan ways of the court. Matthew portrays court life at Herod's birthday party (Mt 14). Needless to say, it lacks high moral standards. Historical sources have also mentioned Herod's participation in pagan worship, another clue to the cultural allurements present in Mary Magdalene's time.

If Bruckberger's theory is correct, it may explain Mary Magdalene's historical association with prostitution and adultery and her association with a town reputed for prostitution and idolatry. Whether true or not, the fact remains that she accompanied Jesus and offered him what she had from her very own means. That would not be the easiest of lifestyles. It would have required a persistent battle against selfishness and self-seeking pleasures. This tension would have been inevitable if she left behind the comforts of home to follow Jesus around Galilee and even to Jerusalem.

The evangelists Mark and Luke offer a clue about the degree of Mary Magdalene's participation within Jesus' closer band of disciples. After listing several women, including Mary Magdalene, Mark mentions that "in Galilee, these women had followed him and cared for his needs" (Mark 15:41). They accompanied Jesus as he traveled from place to place teaching, preaching and healing. A logical deduction is that they were privy to many of his teachings and works. Just how much they were is alluded to in Luke's account of the angel appearing to the women at the empty tomb. The angel says, "Why do you look for the living among the dead? He is not here; he has risen! *Remember how he told you, while he was still with you in Galilee*: 'The Son of Man must be delivered over to the hands of sinners, be crucified and on the third day be raised again'" (Lk 24:5-7). This indicates that the women were part of the band of disciples when Jesus spoke these prophecies.

The women continued to "accompany Jesus" during the early Church period, sharing in the building of God's Kingdom. The Acts of the Apostles gives the account of the early Church's gathering in the upper room and "all joining together constantly in prayer, along with the women…" (Acts 1:14). Luke continues to report, "In those days, Peter stood up among the believers" to announce that it was necessary to choose another to replace Judas. He addressed the group of one hundred twenty believers (Acts 1:15-16). We can imagine Mary Magdalene there in the fervor of the moment, praying for the one chosen to take over the apostolic ministry which Judas left (Acts 1:24-25). Mary's generous support for Jesus, his disciples, and his body, the Church, was more than monetary assistance. Several translations of Luke 8:3 say that the women ministered to them "from their substance." Whether it was property, money, food, prayer, or accompaniment, there is a sense of totality that offers supports and participates in the building of God's Kingdom. And this totality brought her to the foot of the cross.

Salome dancing in Herod's court

# AT THE FOOT OF THE CROSS

## MT. 27:56; MK. 15:40; JN. 19:25; LK. 23:49

All four evangelists mention Mary Magdalene at the foot of the cross. Her presence highlights her fidelity and special closeness to Jesus as well as her strength and endurance. While many fled, she was steadfast, along with other women.

The Gospel remarks that they stood at a distance. They were not permitted to enter the exact area of the crucifixion. A commemorative area within the Holy Sepulcher in Jerusalem enables visitors to imagine the place and distance from which the women were onlookers. It's only about thirty meters from the upper chapel built in the fourth century to commemorate the hill of Calvary to its base. There she could look upon her crucified Savior, hear his words, and watch the redemptive sacrifice of the Son of God.

At the foot of the cross, she did not understand the magnitude of what Jesus was doing. But her presence hints of a steadfast and decisive character. Her heart belonged to Jesus. Human respect played no role in her decision to accompany Jesus in his passion and death. Jesus endured derision; so would she. Mockery and spite did not make her flee. She showed up, and she stayed.

Her action speaks volumes about her magnanimity and inner strength. Her greatness does not lie in power, but in being "a kernel of wheat that falls to the ground and dies" (John 12:24). Mary experienced that internal dying in the furrow. But Jesus also taught that "if the grain falls and dies, it bears much fruit." Certainly, Mary's suffering presence acted as a fruitful grain of sacrifice for the foundation of the Church.

## WITNESS TO THE BURIAL OF JESUS

*MT 27:61; MK 15:47; LK 23:55*

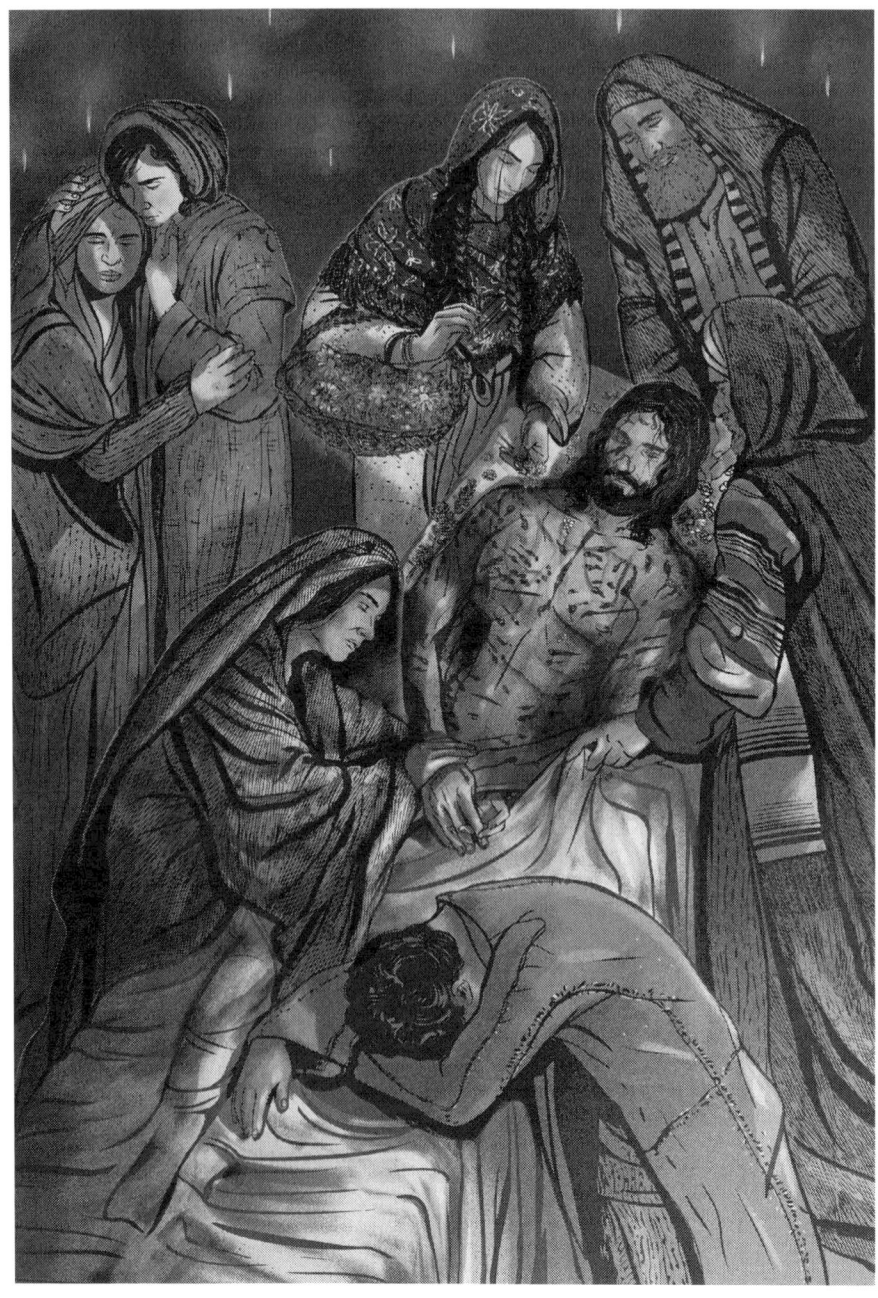

Not only is Mary a witness to Jesus' crucifixion, but also to the lowering of his body from the cross and to his burial in the tomb. All of the evangelists report this fact. John adds an extra element, revealing the women's part in his burial. "They took the body of Jesus and bound it with burial cloths along with the spices, according to Jewish burial custom" (Jn 19:40).

Imagine Mary Magdalene and the other women preparing Jesus for burial, albeit rapidly.[54] Sabbath was swiftly approaching and the custom was to bury the deceased as soon as possible. With what emotion and reverence would they have prepared his body? Did they also gather flowers and place them quickly around his head before they bound his body in the burial cloth and closed the tomb Friday afternoon before Sabbath arrived?

This question arises due to a discovery on the Shroud of Turin.[55] Scientific studies have been carried out on the Shroud, the long piece of fabric that many believe is the actual burial cloth of Jesus. Professor Avinoam Danin, a leading Israeli botanist, identified several species of flowers on the Shroud around the head of the image of the crucified man. It is evident that almost 300 flowers with stems removed were placed around and on the head. Four of the flower types are located primarily within a 6-12 mile radius around Jerusalem and Hebron. Images of ferocious thorns were also identified near the head. Finally, several of the flower species bloom in March and April, the time of Jesus' crucifixion.

The studies bring alive the possible scene only alluded to in the Gospels. The Gospels leave out many details, including their dispositions and conversations on the Sabbath between the crucifixion and the resurrection. One can only imagine the women's anticipation of Sabbath's end so they could return to the tomb. And return, they did.

# WITNESS TO THE EMPTY TOMB

*MT 28:1; MK 16:1-2; JN 20:1-2, 11, 16; LK 24:1-3*

Early Sunday morning, the women made their way to the tomb for better preparation of Jesus' body. The Orthodox Church portrays her in icons with a vessel, calling her the Myrrh-Bearer. But, in the end, there was no need for the burial spices and ointments. They found the tomb empty. What was Mary Magdalene's surprise upon finding the empty tomb? John expresses it best, depicting Mary Magdalene running to Simon Peter and "the other disciple, the one Jesus loved," namely, John (Jn. 20:2). Mary was perplexed at the missing body. She immediately deduced "They have taken the Lord out of the tomb, and we don't know where they have put him" (Jn. 20:2). John did not refer to any other women there, only Mary Magdalene. He specifically gave her credit as the first witness of the empty tomb and to the Risen Jesus.

A twenty first-century mindset can easily pass over this detail, as if it's no big deal that she was a witness. Some scholars claim that women were credible witnesses in the first-century. They mention that Flavius Josephus's accounts of the battles of Masada and Gamla came from the witness of women. But it does give pause, considering that the first witnesses to the greatest event in salvation history, recorded by male disciples, were women, and specifically a woman who at first did not "get it" when she looked upon the empty tomb.

Despite her initial perplexity, Jesus appears to her, revealing his triumph over sin and death. John's gospel beautifully portrays their encounter in which he strengthens her faith and sends her forth as a witness to his resurrection. A further reflection on Jesus' appearance to Mary Magdalene is found in Part Four. In a culture that often invalidated the witness of women, how could this give credibility to the entire claim of Jesus' divinity? Not only are the female witnesses found in all four evangelists, but the evangelists confess the initial disbelief of the Eleven and the other disciples. Mark and Luke report that "when they heard that Jesus was alive and that she had seen him, they did not believe it" (Mk 16:11)... "because their words seemed to them like nonsense" (Luke 24:11). Nonetheless, this does not deter the women's conviction, or their proclamation of what they had witnessed.

# ANNOUNCING THAT JESUS IS RISEN

*JN 20:18; LK 24:9-11; MK 16:10; MT 28:8-10*

Perhaps Mary was disheartened over the apostles' initial disbelief, but she was able to let this go and focus on the more important matter at hand. She had a task, one commissioned by an angel, according to Mark's account. "Go, tell his disciples and Peter, 'He is going ahead of you into Galilee. There you will see him, just as he told you'" (Mk 16:7). Matthew describes the state the women were in after receiving the angel's commission. "They were afraid yet filled with joy and ran to tell his disciples" (Mt 28:8). Imagine Mary's determination, bolstered when she was commissioned not only by an angel but also by Jesus himself. Matthew relates,

> Suddenly Jesus met them. "Greetings," he said. They came to him, clasped his feet and worshipped him. Then Jesus said to them, "Do not be afraid. Go and tell my brothers to go to Galilee; there they will see me"
>
> —Mt 28:9-10

Despite others' disbelief, Mary Magdalene was likely persistent in getting her message across. Perhaps she encouraged them to go and see for themselves and follow Jesus' instructions; consequently, "The eleven disciples went to Galilee, to the mountain where Jesus told them to go" (Mt 28:16).

Mary's powerful witness and essential announcing of the Good News, won her the title *Apostle to the Apostles*. This title goes back to a Church Father named Hippolytus of Rome. He lived from approximately 170-236 AD. Hippolytus was in a line of disciples leading back to John the Evangelist. He followed Irenaeus, who was a disciple of Polycarp, a disciple of John. The Orthodox Christian church offers her a similar title, *Equal to the Apostles*.

Her role in this extraordinary event won her a place in the highest liturgical celebration in the Church: Easter Sunday. A medieval hymn is proclaimed or sung before the Gospel, remembering Mary Magdalene's Easter proclamation.

Christians, to the Paschal Victim, Offer your thankful praises!

A Lamb the sheep redeems: Christ, who only is sinless,

Reconciles sinners to the Father.

Death and life have contended in that combat stupendous:

The Prince of life, who died, reigns immortal.

Speak, Mary, declaring What you saw, wayfaring.

"The tomb of Christ, who is living,

The glory of Jesus' resurrection;

Bright angels attesting, The shroud and napkin resting.

Yes, my Christ my hope is arisen:

To Galilee he goes before you."

Christ indeed from death is risen,

our new life obtaining.

Have mercy, victor King, ever reigning!

Amen. Alleluia.[56]

# PART III: THE MYSTERY OF MARY MAGDALENE

*Insights from Historical Traditions*

---

As stories are passed on and recounted through the centuries, certain features of a person's life take form. Sometimes characteristics of the person begin to merge with other historical figures. Traits and incidents are embellished or recast from a new perspective. Intertwining and contrasting ideas create confusion about the actual story of the original person in question.

Mary Magdalene is the perfect example. Contradictory stories abound and have created debates about the real Mary Magdalene up until the present day. Historical narratives of the life and character of Mary Magdalene have taken shape through the influence of cultural contexts, philosophical and political agendas, theological reflection, and spiritual or pastoral intentions.

Nonetheless, when doing a general survey of multiple sources, common characteristics begin to emerge. Perhaps these are clues to the authentic Mary Magdalene. An influential woman begins to appear. While she may have been an influential woman before she met Jesus, the brilliance of her story was born from the redeeming and transforming love of Jesus. By gleaning common character traits from some sources outside the Canonical Gospels and reflecting on her role in the history of salvation, her legacy comes to light. Her legacy continues to resound to the present day, allowing us to reflect more profoundly on the mystery of redemption and the dynamics of the Christian life.

## APOCRYPHAL GOSPELS (GNOSTIC TEXTS)

The Apocryphal Gospels, or Gnostic texts, are not accepted in the Canonical Scriptures as a part of Christian revelation due to their later dating and their unchristian content. There are, however, some compatible characteristics between the Mary Magdalene portrayed in the Gnostic texts and assumptions made from the Canonical Gospels: her leadership among leaders, her wisdom, and her special bond with Jesus in which she is his close disciple and learner. The Gnostic gospels that refer to Mary, believed to be written around the 2nd to 5th centuries, are part of larger collections of ancient documents. Among them, those that may refer to Mary Magdalene are the *Pistis Sophia*; *the Dialogue of the Savior*; and the *Gospels* of Mary, Philip, and Thomas.

It is important to understand the "Gnostic lens" and why these books did not get incorporated into the approved canon of revealed scripture in the early Church. The Gnostic texts rewrote the Christian Gospels with a twist of Platonic philosophy, Egyptian mythology, and esoteric teachings. Some of the Gnostic teachings and the underlining messages stray far from Jesus' messages in the Canonical Gospels. Gnosticism offers a dualistic worldview that pits the spiritual against the material realm. Gnostics believe that God created the spiritual world, but a demi-god is responsible for the evil material world. Matter, such as the human body, is believed to be inherently evil. Hence in one Gnostic Gospel, Jesus recommends to men not to pray in the same place as women and to get rid of women's work (child-bearing) because it brings physical reality into the world.[57]

Gnosticism also prides itself on the attainment of *gnosis* or "secret knowledge," claiming that the way of salvation is knowledge, and anyone who acquires a higher knowledge is part of the elite. There are traces of Gnosticism throughout the pre-Christian era among the ancient Babylonian civilization, through early Egyptian Christian formation, into St. Augustine's days with the Manicheans, and up to present day modern new-age movements.[58] Ultimately, it denied both Jesus' humanity and divinity and was hence, condemned by the early Church leaders. Despite this, they are addressed here to acquire clarity about the false assumptions derived from these texts, as well as to glean characteristics of Mary's personality that complement the canonical texts. While they cannot be counted on as a source of revelation, some dates and facts within the Gnostic texts may offer a window into some aspects of the oral tradition of the early Church.

## THE GNOSTIC GOSPEL OF PHILLIP

The Nag Hammadi collection, found in 1945 in Egypt, contained the Coptic versions of the Dialogue of the Savior and the Gnostic Gospels of Phillip and Thomas. The *Gospel of Phillip* played a prominent role in the *Da Vinci Code* story. In short, Dan Brown's novel presented Jesus and Mary Magdalene as married. She bore Jesus' child and fled to Gaul, modern-day southern France. *The Da Vinci Code* claims that their bloodline continued through the Merovingian dynasty (French royalty) until the present day. The book plays off of a 1960s claim by a con-man in France who said that he was the rightful heir to the throne of France and a direct descendant of Jesus and Mary Magdalene. Serious scholars laugh at this fiction claiming fact, for there is no mention of, or context for, Jesus' marriage in either canonical or non-canonical gospels.[59]

What is evident is that Mary Magdalene and other women accompanied Jesus, as Luke 8:2 testifies. The *Gospel of Phillip* mentions Mary Magdalene twice, referring to her as Jesus' "companion." The original Coptic word borrows from a Greek word, *koinônos*, meaning "associate," not "spouse" as is sometimes interpreted.

> There were three who always walked with the Lord: Mary his mother and her sister and Magdalene, the one who was called his companion… (they) were each a Mary.

Another passage, full of missing parts, reads:

> And a companion of the *[gap]* Mary Magdalene. *[gap]* her more than *[gap]* the disciples *[gap]* kiss her *[gap]* on her *[gap]*.

While there are many gaps, some interpret the text as alluding to sexual intimacy. Interpretations as such place a contemporary hyper-sexualized cultural construct on this passage, and ignore the historical and philosophical context. The "kiss" may infer a common form of greeting or the spiritual transmission of knowledge. St Paul says three times in his letters, "Greet one another with a holy kiss." The Middle Eastern culture continues today to make use of the kiss as a greeting.

Furthermore, within the Gnostic worldview, the kiss can symbolize the transmission of *gnosis* or "secret knowledge." In another excerpt, Jesus speaks of a spiritual sonship and fatherhood and of the way that truth is passed on, giving spiritual life to another. He says to his disciples,

> For it is by a kiss that the perfect conceive and give birth. For this reason, we also kiss one another. We receive conception from the grace that is in one another.

The early Christian Church, outside of Gnosticism, had a similar understanding. Truth passes from person to person by way of the mouth. And truth offers life. It is, in a mystical sense, a way of conceiving or giving birth to spiritual sons and daughters. Far from alluding to sexual intimacy, the kiss of Jesus to Mary Magdalene reveals the general belief of this woman's giftedness and special knowledge that she transmits to others. The canonical gospels reveal essentially the same idea: her privileged role as a transmitter of the culminating event in the life of Jesus and pinnacle of Christian revelation, his triumph over sin and death through his resurrection. Henceforth, all may enter the gateway to eternal life, through Jesus Christ.

## THE GNOSTIC GOSPEL OF THOMAS

The Gnostic *Gospel of Thomas* also refers to Mary Magdalene. Reading some of its passages with a twenty-first-century mental construct could create a war of the sexes. Here is one such case in verse 114:

> Simon Peter said to them, "Make Mary leave us, for females don't deserve life."
>
> Jesus said, "Look, I will guide her to make her *male*, so that she too may become a living spirit resembling you *males*. For every *female* who makes herself *male* will enter the Kingdom of Heaven." [emphasis added]

It is necessary to step into the ancient mindset of gender to understand why a woman would have to become a "man." In the Gnostic worldview, influenced by Platonic philosophy, creation is an emanation from God, and all is evolving towards its fullness. Maleness was higher on the spectrum and represented power and strength. The sexual act revealed his power since man was considered to be the one who dominated the act, whereas the woman was the recipient and the one dominated.

Even within the early Christian writings accepted by the Church, we see the concept of women being the "weaker sex," but with an altogether different foundational concept of sexuality. From a Christian perspective, there is no need to be liberated from "being woman." A truly Christian worldview perceives the creation of the human person as essentially male or female, equal in dignity while complementary in ways of being. In the ancient Gnostic worldview, prevalent also in some contemporary cultural currents, gender is seen as a continuum, rather than a "being male" or "being female." Consequently, in the passage above, a woman would be seen as "an imperfect man," whose first step is to "make herself male." The process of salvation for the Gnostic mindset was to overcome ignorance, first becoming "male" and thus living within a higher spiritual realm, eventually transcending even the limits of mortality.[60]

Thomas McDaniel, a scripture scholar, offers another interpretation of this passage from the Gnostic *Gospel of Thomas*. His etymological interpretation takes the reader away from a face-value translation through a word analysis. McDaniel believes that the Gnostic text came from a translation of the *Vorlage*, an ancient text that no longer exists. Ambiguities in words brought about a change in meaning. Since the Hebrew/Aramaic cognates of "male" are ambiguous in their meanings, this led to a Gnostic interpretation that promoted an agenda which deprecated women. In a new interpretation, McDaniel offers a connotation of Mary Magdalene being a remembrance and someone who receives salvation because of her repentance and obedience.

He argues that behind the Coptic word "male" (*hooit*), occurring three times in this text, is a Hebrew, Aramaic, and Arabic word, *zahar* or *dakara*. *Dakara* can mean either (1) "male, male organ" or (2) "remembrance, memory." If "male" is indeed referring to her as a remembrance, it echoes Matthew 26:13. Jesus says, "Truly I tell you, wherever this Gospel is preached throughout the world, what she has done will also be told, *in memory of her.*" The unnamed woman in that passage refers to Mary of Bethany, who anoints Jesus. A further historical association turns Mary of Bethany into Mary of Magdala, hence Mary of Magdala becomes associated with the "anointer." In this context, Mary is a "remembrance" or witness to others.

The Arabic *dakara* also has the connotation of repentance and obedience. With this Arabic cognate in focus, the words used in verse 114 could have meant that Jesus would lead Mary to *repentance* and *obedience*, "promising that any repentant woman could enter the kingdom as readily as any male penitent—thereby dismissing Peter's chauvinistic request."[61] This idea corroborates a long-held tradition that Mary was a repentant sinner. Interpreting the text as such brings into focus the gift Jesus offered to Mary Magdalene at her conversion. The seven demons were not an impediment. Through a spirit of repentance, Jesus was able to guide her into the Kingdom of Heaven. McDaniel's interpretation broadens the scope of salvation to include men and women alike.

## THE GNOSTIC GOSPEL OF MARY

The Gnostic *Gospel of Mary* was discovered in 1896 in northern Egypt and was part of a fifth-century Coptic codex. Mary Magdalene is not named specifically, but "Mary" is assumed to be she. The text of the Gospel of Mary was missing pages 1-6 and pages 11-14. However, a fragment from what remained reveals Mary's possible leadership among the first followers of Jesus. If read with the sentiments of the Canonical Gospels, the Gospel of Mary matches it with Jesus' love for Mary, her acknowledgment of the wonders Jesus has done for her, and her proclamation of a mystery. It tells the story of the apostles grieving and worrying about their duty to preach to the Gentiles. Mary consoles and motivates them, saying,

> (Mary): "Let us praise His greatness, for He has prepared us and made us into Men."
>
> Peter says to Mary: "Sister, we know that the Savior loved you more than the rest of the women."
>
> Mary said, "What is hidden to you I will proclaim to you."

Then Mary begins to teach them. The final dialogue is an argument about whether or not they should believe her. Peter and Andrew do not want to. Levi (Matthew) defends her, and they finally go out and begin to preach.

As mentioned previously, "being made into Men" connotes a spiritual ascendency within the Gnostic philosophical context. Mary expresses their maturity in knowledge of the mysteries Jesus left them to ponder. This "coming into the light" reflects the multiple places in the Canonical Scriptures, particularly in the Acts of the Apostles, in which Jesus' disciples received the gift of understanding. They finally came to the realization of what Jesus had done for all and began to preach, despite the consequences and persecution.

This passage, however, is often used to allude to jealousy that may have existed within the early Church among male leaders toward Mary Magdalene's influence. The extent of the controversy is uncertain. Universal human experiences give evidence of the challenges among the most well-meaning Church leaders to "get along" and see eye to eye on every matter concerning the particularities of shepherding a flock. Conflicts, pride, and misunderstandings exist among the best-intentioned peoples. In this life, human imperfections within a divine project are integral to the building of the Kingdom of God. Imperfections and challenges only reinforce the need for the message that Mary Magdalene first proclaimed. They remind us that building the Kingdom of God is a task beyond our human capabilities and that God can work despite our sinfulness and weaknesses.

Jesus' resurrection is a sign of the newness of life available to all and points to a future restoration. Until Jesus' final coming, when God will be all in all, the human journey is like a pilgrimage. It belongs to both men and women to purify the mind and heart and strive to build the Kingdom of God with the help of God's grace. Men and women alike rely on God's mercy and forgiveness, available to us thanks to Jesus' sacrifice and resurrection. His mercy comes to the aid of injustices caused by envy or pride that mingle within the human condition. Saint Paul referred to the challenges facing the early Christian communities among classes, ethnicities, and the sexes. Mary Magdalene and the early disciples likely sought and struggled to discern God's will and remain united in the Holy Spirit. This reality check is necessary for ongoing purification and maturing of those within leadership as well as those among the flock.

Mary's role as wise teacher, within this particular text, corresponds to her title as "Apostle to the Apostles" in the early Church. Her personality traits as a leader among leaders and her special intimacy with Jesus come to the forefront. Rereading the Canonical Gospel accounts in light of the apocryphal texts reinforces those characteristics. She is among the intimate band of disciples who accompany Jesus throughout Galilee. She remains his faithful disciple all the way to the foot of the cross. And Jesus designates her as the first spokesperson to reveal the essential salvific message to his apostles. While fantastical assumptions abound from interpretations of the apocryphal texts, the real Mary Magdalene is still perceptible amidst the reconstructed gospel stories.

## CHURCH FATHERS

The Church Fathers[62] were key contributors to a discernment process when questionable doctrines arose. Gnosticism was one of those "questionables." They discerned that it contradicted and misread Christ's legacy. Thanks, however, to those types of confrontations and the early Church's reflections on revelation, doctrinal points and spiritual and theological gems came to light for future generations.

The Church Fathers, like the Gnostics, take up the theme of special intimacy between Jesus and Mary Magdalene, but in light of the bigger picture of salvation history. For the Church Fathers, the Scriptures recount the saving plan of God in which Jesus reconciles us and the world through his life, death, and resurrection. The Gospel stories for them are not mere fiction or symbolic actions, but a testimony of the salvific action of God at work in the world. All is recapitulated in Jesus Christ, the Son of God. He became what we are, in all things but sin, while not changing his being as a divine person. In this way, he reconciles all, uniting humanity to God. The drama of salvation involves a gift and the acceptance of that gift through faith and the free human response.

In this light, for the Church Fathers, Mary Magdalene becomes a model of the power of faith that leads to a transformation from sinfulness to holiness, from vice to virtue. She becomes a beacon of hope through her sincerity and deep-seated conviction, exemplifying the drama of redemption played out within the individual, the Church, and all of humanity.

In the period of the Church Fathers there is also much reflection on the person of Jesus Christ who fulfills what was alluded to in the past, while at the same time, shedding light on the future reality still to come. They illustrated these connections with allegories and analogies between the Hebrew Scriptures (the Old Testament) and the Gospel accounts. The third-century theologian and bishop Hippolytus of Rome offers a prime example.

### HIPPOLYTUS (THIRD CENTURY): THE BRIDE & SPOUSE

Hippolytus brings together John's account of Mary's searching for Jesus near the empty tomb and the familiar scriptural poem, the Song of Songs. While his analogy makes use of the debatable association between Mary of Magdala and Mary of Bethany, it also accentuates the spousal nature of Mary Magdalene's relationship with Jesus, in the spiritual sense. Through this type of reflection, Mary Magdalene becomes a bride and spouse. In his work, Hippolytus personifies the Gospel figures of Martha and Mary of Bethany as the icons of the "zealous synagogue." They are expectant brides longing for the bridegroom.

> 'By night, I sought him whom my soul loveth': See how this is fulfilled in Martha and Mary. In their figure, zealous Synagogue sought the dead Christ…for she teaches us and tells us: By night I sought him whom my soul loveth.

Martha and Mary are the "zealous synagogue," the bride or people who search for the apparently "dead" Christ. They search in the dark of night, meaning that they are in pursuit of the one for whom they long. In the Christian worldview, Jesus is the expected bridegroom; and those who are in search of him are a type of bride. By associating Mary with the figure of a bride, she also becomes a figure of the Church: a community of believers in search of the bridegroom, the Messiah. The nuptial union established on earth through faith will reach its consummation in the end times when "God will be all in all" (1 Cor 15:28). Until that time, their faith and love spur them on as they search for their beloved.

The concept of a spiritual espousal is difficult to grasp in contemporary culture, but has its place in Christian theology, especially in the Catholic Church. Religious and consecrated persons, women especially, and even some women from other Christian communities, perceive their commitment to God in light of a "spousal relationship with Jesus Christ." Mary Magdalene becomes for them a model of persevering faith and passionate love, making their relationship with Jesus the primacy of their apostolic action and missionary drive.

### GREGORY OF NYSSA (FOURTH CENTURY): MODEL OF FAITH

Gregory of Nyssa marvels at the fact that a woman first announced Jesus' work of redemption. At the same time he points out how appropriate that is in the full light of salvation history. He connects Eve and Mary Magdalene. By Mary Magdalene's proclamation, she reverses the transgression of Eve. Through Eve, one woman's disobedience ushered in the beginning of evil among the human race. But now, through Mary Magdalene's proclamation of the Good News, Eve's initial proclamation is annulled. Eve's words originally sought to tempt man to choose self over God. Mary's faithful proclamation of the resurrection opens the door for Jesus to redeem previous transgressions. In this way, she becomes a model of the power of faith that ushers in the redemptive grace won by Jesus. Gregory continues his reflection by stressing the life-changing message behind her "glad tidings" that continues resounding to all who become disciples of Jesus.

> And these glad tidings He proclaims through the woman, not to those disciples only, but also to all who up to the present day become disciples of the Word, — the tidings, namely, that man is no longer outlawed, nor cast out of the Kingdom of God, but is once more a son... He who for our sakes was partaker of flesh and blood has recovered you, and brought you back to the place whence ye strayed away, becoming mere flesh and blood by sin. And so He from whom we were formerly alienated by our revolt has become our Father and our God.[63]

The message that Mary Magdalene proclaims seems so simple, yet it acts as an open-door invitation to an entirely new life.

### SAINT JEROME (FOURTH CENTURY): MODEL OF VIRTUE

In addition to highlighting the tremendous role Mary plays through faith and proclamation, the Church Fathers also extolled her virtues. In the fourth century, St. Jerome wrote a letter in memory of a virtuous woman named Marcela. In it, he references the virtues of Mary Magdalene.

> The unbelieving reader may perhaps laugh at me for dwelling so long on the praises of mere women; yet if he will but remember how holy women followed our Lord and Saviour and ministered to Him of their substance, and how the three Marys stood before the cross and especially how *Mary Magdalene — called the tower from the earnestness and glow of her faith —* was privileged to see the rising Christ first of all before the very apostles, he will convict himself of pride sooner than me of folly. For we judge of people's virtue not by their sex but by their character and hold those to be worthy of the highest glory who have renounced both rank and wealth.[64] [emphasis added]

Jerome calls Mary the tower, indicating a nickname given to her for her character traits and that stretches back to the meaning of the word Magdala. He stresses that virtue is more important than one's sex or social status. A question remains: Is Jerome making a comparison between Marcela and Mary Magdalene when he refers to those who renounced both rank and wealth? If so, this reinforces the belief that Mary Magdalene was indeed ranked within the early Church as a woman associated with the elite and wealthy.

### EPHREM OF SYRIA (FOURTH CENTURY): IMPORTANT ROLE OF WOMEN & SPIRITUAL MOTHERHOOD

A fourth-century Syrian poet, deacon, and theologian, Ephrem was proclaimed a Doctor of the Church by the Catholic Church and is counted as a Venerable Father by the Orthodox Church. In one of his poems, he presents women who played a part in the two most important moments in salvation history: the incarnation and the resurrection. Mary, the Virgin Mother, received Jesus in her womb. Mary, the Magdalene, was witness to the empty tomb. These two Marys are present at the beginning and the end.

> At the beginning of his coming to earth, A virgin was first to receive him,
> And at the raising up from the grave, To a woman he showed his
>      resurrection.
> In his beginning and in his fulfillment
> The name of his mother cries out and is present
> *Mary received him by conception*
> *And saw an angel at his grave.* [emphasis added]

When interpreting Ephrem's poetic purposefulness, two themes surface: woman's essential role and spiritual motherhood. The last two lines poetically weave together the two Marys (Jesus' Mother and Mary Magdalene) and the important role they played in the physical and spiritual sense. Without the incarnation (the Son of God's taking on human nature) and the resurrection (Jesus' overcoming the powers of sin and death), there would be no Christianity, no definitive redemption.

While Mary, the Mother of Jesus, conceives and gives birth to Jesus physically, the poem seems to merge the two women into one by the end. By analogy, we can say that Mary Magdalene "conceives" and "gives birth to Jesus" through faith.[65] Her faith in his resurrection bears fruit in bringing the Good News of salvation to others, opening up the possibility of Christ's life within all those who welcome the gospel message. Preaching, teaching, and sharing the Good News leads to new life and an extension of God's Kingdom. Women play a tremendous role by transmitting their living faith as mothers, catechists, teachers, and friends.

In the Christian worldview, all women, as well as men, have the possibility of "giving birth to Jesus" through faith.  Men and women become spiritual mothers and fathers when they dedicate their time and lives to accompanying others in their faith journey, helping others to grow in their life of grace and friendship with Jesus Christ. Among spiritual mothers and fathers are those especially dedicated totally to God through celibacy. Mary Magdalene becomes a model for celibates and those dedicated to ministry. Like Mary Magdalene, through a passionate love for Jesus and witness to his resurrection, women bear fruit in the spiritual realm as "mother."

## GREGORY THE GREAT (SIXTH CENTURY): MARY AS THE RECIPIENT OF MERCIFUL LOVE & MODEL OF PERSEVERANCE

In the sixth century, Gregory the Great sent a letter of encouragement to a woman named Gregoria. Gregoria had written a list of sinful accusations against herself. In response, Gregory used Mary Magdalene as a role model to encourage her to take heart, for God's mercy is upon those who ardently love the Lord. To make his point he associated Mary Magdalene with Mary of Bethany and the sinful woman who anoints Jesus' feet. In his reflection, he contrasts Eve's first sin with the triumph over sin that Mary Magdalene proclaims. Her profound internal experience of Jesus conquering her heart with his mercy gives credence to her proclamation. Mary Magdalene's experience of the Lord's merciful gesture of redemption fulfills an Old Testament prophecy at work, not only in her, but in all the Church.

> *And this was by the wonderful dispensation of the loving-kindness of God, that life should be announced by a woman's mouth, because by a woman's mouth had been the first taste of death in Paradise. And at another time also, with another Mary, she saw the Lord after his resurrection, and held his feet. Bring before your eyes, I pray you, what hands held whose feet. That woman who had been a sinner in the city, those hands which had been polluted with iniquity, touched the feet of him who sits at the right hand of the Father above all the angels. Let us estimate, if we can, what those bowels of heavenly loving-kindness are, that a woman who had been plunged through sin into the whirlpool's depth should be thus lifted high on the wing of love through grace. It is fulfilled, sweet daughter, it is fulfilled, what was promised to us by the prophetic voice concerning this time of the holy Church: "And in that day the house of David shall be an open fountain for ablution of the sinner, and of her that is unclean" (Zechariah 13:1). For the house of David is an open fountain for ablution to us sinners, because we are washed from the filth of our iniquities by mercy now disclosed through the son of David our Savior.[66]*

In yet another reflection, titled Homily 25, Gregory invites his listeners to ponder Mary's attitude as she stands outside the empty tomb. He sets her up as a model of perseverance. His lengthy explanation ponders the holy desires that God himself plants within the soul and how Jesus' love for each person prompts a search for him. The text follows:

*We should reflect on Mary's attitude and the great love she felt for Christ; for though the disciples had left the tomb, she remained. She was still seeking the one she had not found, and while she sought she wept; burning with the fire of love, she longed for him whom she thought had been taken away. And so it happened that the woman who stayed behind to seek Christ was the only one to see him. For perseverance is essential to any good deed, as the voice of truth tells us: "Whoever perseveres to the end will be saved."[67]

At first she sought but did not find, but when she persevered it happened that she found what she was looking for. When our desires are not satisfied, they grow stronger, and becoming stronger they take hold of their object. Holy desires likewise grow with anticipation, and if they do not grow they are not really desires. Anyone who succeeds in attaining the truth has burned with such a great love. As David says: "My soul has thirsted for the living God; when shall I come and appear before the face of God?" And so also in the Song of Songs the Church says: I was wounded by love; and again: "My soul is melted with love. Woman, why are you weeping? Whom do you seek? " She is asked why she is sorrowing so that her desire might be strengthened; for when she mentions whom she is seeking, her love is kindled all the more ardently.

Jesus says to her: "Mary." Jesus is not recognized when he calls her "woman"; so he calls her by name, as though he were saying: Recognize me as I recognize you; for I do not know you as I know others; I know you as yourself. And so Mary, once addressed by name, recognizes who is speaking. She immediately calls him *rabboni*, that is to say, "teacher," because the one whom she sought outwardly was the one who inwardly taught her to keep on searching.

## THE GREAT DEBATE

### WILL THE REAL MARY MAGDALENE PLEASE STAND UP?

In the controversial homily 33, Gregory the Great expressed the popularly held belief of the Occidental church of his days: that Mary of Magdala was the sinful woman who anointed Jesus' feet and also Mary of Bethany. He wrote, "She whom Luke calls the sinful woman, whom John calls Mary, we believe to be the Mary from whom seven devils were ejected according to Mark." An analysis of several passages follows:

- *Luke 7:36-38:* Luke names a "sinful woman" who anoints Jesus' feet in Simon the Pharisee's house. (From the placement of this passage, many assume that this takes place in Galilee.)

- *John: 12:1-8:* John names Mary who anoints Jesus' feet in Bethany.

- *Matthew 26:6-13:* This text is similar to John 12:1-8; however, Matthew names the house as Simon the Leper's in Bethany. Some conclude that John's account of the anointing may be the same one, and that Simon is the father of Lazarus, Martha, and Mary of Bethany.

- *Mark 16:9:* Mark names Mary Magdalene as the one Jesus appeared to first, "Mary Magdalene, out of whom he had cast seven devils."

Luke and John tell the story of a woman who anoints Jesus. The two accounts seem to take place in different venues: Bethany near Jerusalem and Galilee in Simon the Pharisee's house. John's account of Mary anointing Jesus' feet in the house in Bethany brings about the association that Mary Magdalene's sister is Martha. Luke's account simply mentions the woman as the one whose sins are forgiven, yet the details are similar in some aspects. (See Appendix A for a comparative chart of the anointings.) By associating Luke and John's account as the same women, Gregory the Great asserts that Mary of Bethany (also assumed to be Mary of Magdala) is the sinful woman. Reading beyond Luke's account offers another association. Directly after telling the story of the sinful woman anointing Jesus' feet, he mentions the women disciples following Jesus (Luke 8:1-3). Among them, Mary of Magdala is helping them with her resources. The question arises: how could that sinful woman afford such an expensive ointment? Was that sinful woman wealthy? Was it Mary of Magdala who then follows Jesus, providing for him from her sustenance, a sustenance she had just used to anoint Jesus?

This identification of the sinful women with Mary of Bethany and Mary of Magdala is common within the Occidental (Western) Church tradition; whereas the Oriental Orthodox (Eastern) traditions tend to identify these women as three separate people. The debate has been a long-enduring one.[68] By the ninth century, the Western Church, for the most part, universally accepted the tradition that all three are the same Mary of Magdala. A rejection of this tradition came with the sixteenth century Protestant Reformation. Another wave of rejection of the "3-in-1 theory", or *composite Magdalene*, came through twentieth-century biblical scholars. In light of that discussion, the Catholic Liturgy refocused its approach in 1969. The liturgical prayers on the feast day of Mary Magdalene reflect her role as the first witness of the resurrection and her persevering love as she clung to Jesus before being sent to proclaim the Good News of his resurrection (John 20). The prayers dropped her identification with Mary of Bethany and the "woman with the alabaster jar." It is interesting to note that no particular memorial day is offered by the Catholic Church for Mary of Bethany, leaving the association open for pondering. On the other hand, her sister, Martha of Bethany, is specifically commemorated on July 29 for her homage of love for Jesus through her hospitality and her proclamation of Jesus as the Christ, the Son of God.

## THE REPENTANT SINNER REREAD IN THE LIGHT OF THE FEMININE GENIUS

Many accuse Gregory of defaming Mary Magdalene in this homily by calling her a prostitute. Some currents within contemporary feminism attempt to liberate Mary Magdalene from this reputation and reclaim her as a model of an early church leader fighting against a chauvinistic male-dominated leadership. It calls to mind a general sense of women's secondary role within a hierarchical and institutional Church throughout history all the way back to the Gnostic Gospels' allusion to the apostles' jealousy toward Mary due to her favored position and deeper understanding of the Jesus' teachings.

While the accusation against Gregory the Great continues, he does not specifically name her as a prostitute. He does, however, paint the picture of a sinful woman whose life had totally changed. What she once used for vice, she now uses for virtue. Gregory most likely sought to inspire hope through a spirit of repentance, rather than giving Mary a bad name. Mary Magdalene is set up as a repentant sinner who experiences a deep transformation through her encounter with the Lord. When analyzing the passage in light of its content and pastoral context, a new reading surfaces. Her "feminine genius" shines forth.[69] In the passage that follows, he refers to the conversion of at least six vices: greed, lust, envy, vanity, pride, and anger or disrespect. The vices possibly alluded to are inserted in parentheses.

❝And what did these seven devils signify, if not the vices?...

It is clear, brothers, that the woman previously used the unguent to perfume her flesh in forbidden acts. (Greed)

What she therefore displayed more scandalously (Lust), she was now offering to God in a more praiseworthy manner.

She had coveted with earthly eyes (*Envy*), but now through penitence, these are consumed with tears.

She displayed her hair to set off her face (*Vanity*), but now her hair dries her tears.

She had spoken proud things with her mouth (*Pride*), but in kissing the Lord's feet, she now planted her mouth on the Redeemer's feet. For every delight, therefore, she had had in herself, she now immolated herself.

She turned the mass of her crimes to virtues, to serve God entirely, in penance, for as much as she had wrongly held God in contempt. (*Anger*)

Mary Magdalene's plight and transformation echo the history of an idolatrous and sinful nation called to be an example, yet who continually fell away from the Lord. It echoes the prophetic writings of Hosea, called to marry a prostitute and adulteress as a sign of God mercifully forgiving us our infidelities. Through his merciful and gratuitous gesture, he redeems her. It echoes the profound need for redemption experienced by all. In this light, another feminist perspective emerges upon reading Gregory the Great's text. When a woman lives fully aware of her redeemed state, she is receptive to God's continual action within her. She is open to the possibility of a spiritual and holistic liberation. What she once used for self-idolatry and mere human gratification can now be offered for the praise and glory of God. Gregory the Great portrays the "feminine genius" at its best.

Her feminine genius shines forth in the sincere gift of herself to Jesus. Through his initiative and life-giving gift, she is a redeemed person. Now her beauty, her attraction, and her capacity to speak "proud things," can be offered with a pure and sincere heart. Her unique possessions, as a woman, become jewels to offer the Lord. She becomes an icon of hope for women trapped in living as an object for another's pleasure. She becomes a model for a new way of life through an authentic self-giving to God.

### UPGRADING AND REFOCUSING: A RECIPIENT OF JESUS' MERCIFUL LOVE

In 2016, Pope Francis decided to promulgate Mary Magdalene's evident role as "Apostle to the Apostles" during the Year of Mercy. He "upgraded" the liturgical celebration of July 22 from the level of a "memorial day" to a "feast day." This change in the liturgical status puts the celebration on equal footing with the male apostles commemorated throughout the year. Archbishop Arthur Roche, secretary of the Congregation for Divine Worship, wrote that this day calls all Christians to "reflect more deeply on the dignity of women, the new evangelization, and the greatness of the mystery of divine mercy... Pope Francis has taken this decision precisely in the context of the Jubilee of Mercy to highlight the relevance of this woman who showed great love for Christ and was much loved by Christ."[70]

This commemoration helps Christians to reflect on Mary Magdalene's importance in the light of redemption. She is the recipient of Jesus' merciful love that transforms a person into his witness. The Archbishop also pointed out that "Saint Mary Magdalene is an example of true and authentic evangelization, that is, an evangelizer who proclaims the joyful central message of Easter."[71] Hence, whether Mary Magdalene was also Mary of Bethany and the sinful woman who anoints Jesus' feet, they all serve to point the way to the truth of Jesus' ever-present mercy.

## A PROPHETESS: JESUS' ANOINTER?

The question continues to surface as to whether or not Mary Magdalene is the woman who anointed Jesus' feet with the expensive ointment. Associating her as such, however, can help to reflect her role in the mystery of God's saving plan. She takes on an important role as Prophetess, once again, proclaiming the Good News, this time through her prophetic gestures. John's account takes place six days before Passover, the commemoration of the Jewish people's liberation from slavery and entrance to the Promised Land. Jesus fulfills what the first Passover prefigured. He is the "New" Moses. Through his sacrificial death, he redeems humankind from slavery, the slavery of sin. Mary's act is a pre-anointing of Jesus' body before his sacrificial death on the cross. Matthew recounts the same anointing in Bethany.[72] In his account, Jesus said, "When she poured this perfume on my body, she did it to prepare me for burial."

Mary's prophetic act testifies that Jesus is the Messiah-King, set apart for the consummation of the mission that awaits him at the cross and through the resurrection. Throughout the history of the Jewish people, anointing was a sign of election by God. Prophets, priests, and kings received an anointing, or consecration, for their mission. Jesus, as the Son of God, was sent by the Father for his salvific mission. A king had the responsibility of providing for those in his kingdom and, when necessary, redeeming them. Jesus did just that

Cathedral of the Immaculate Conception, Kansas City, MO

by his sacrificial death. Later Mary will confirm with words what the anointer prophetically proclaimed with the gesture of anointing. As a witness of the resurrection, she points to the Messiah-King who conquered sin and death, redeemed humanity, and opened the way to an eternal and Heavenly Kingdom.

## AFTER THE RESURRECTION: TO FRANCE, ROME, & EPHESUS?

Neither the New Testament nor the Church Fathers allude to Mary Magdalene's fate after the resurrection. Likely, she was among the one hundred twenty in the upper room, participating in the beginnings of the early Church formation. Beyond that, different traditions offer possibilities about how her life continued: she traveled to Rome to speak to Caesar; she escaped Christian persecution and ended up in Gaul (present day Southern France); she followed St. John and Jesus' mother to Ephesus. Despite contradictory stories, predominant themes emerge once again. Above all, she continues to be Jesus' faithful disciple announcing the Good News, particularly to leaders.

### ROME: APPEALING TO CAESAR

According to one tradition, after Jesus' ascension into heaven, Mary Magdalene, a wealthy and influential woman, boldly presented herself to Emperor Tiberius Caesar in Rome. The apocryphal Gospel of Nicodemus puts the intention to visit Caesar on the lips of Mary Magdalene herself.

❝Mary Magdalene said, weeping: "Hear, O peoples, tribes, and tongues, and learn to what death the lawless Jews have delivered him who did them ten thousand good deeds. Hear, and be astonished. Who will let these things be heard by all the world? I shall go alone to Rome, to the Caesar. I shall show him what evil Pilate hath done in obeying the lawless Jews." Likewise also, Joseph lamented, saying: "Ah, me! sweetest Jesus, most excellent of men, if indeed it be proper to call thee man, who hast wrought such miracles as no man has ever done. How shall I enshroud thee? How shall I entomb thee?"[73]

The scholarly opinion about this text is that it is a fabricated story, written from a Christian viewpoint, and responding to a pagan document entitled *The Acts of Pontius Pilate*. The text's origin is anywhere from the third to the fifth century. It reflects sentiments of the writer towards both Pontius Pilate and the "lawless Jews" for being responsible for the death of an innocent man.

The possibility that Mary Magdalene presented herself to Tiberius Caesar in Rome is questionable, as the date of his retirement to the island of Capri may have been before the death of Jesus.[74]

In the Orthodox tradition, the story continues. When Mary Magdalene announces that Jesus is risen, the emperor, mocking her, said that Jesus had no more risen than the egg in her hand was red. Immediately, the egg turned red as a sign from God to illustrate the truth of her message. Mary, in turn, preached the Good News to the imperial household. The Emperor then heeded her complaints about Pilate condemning an innocent man to death and had Pilate removed from Jerusalem. Some authors have attributed St. Paul's reference to Mary as signifying this event. In his letter to the Romans, he says, "Greet Mary, who labored much for us" (Romans 16:6). It is true that Caesar removed Pilate from Jerusalem around the year 36 AD. From Flavius Josephus's perspective, however, it was punishment for his violent reaction to the Samaritan uprising.[75]

Art work depicts Mary Magdalene with a red Easter egg in her hand. An ancient Greek manuscript, kept in the monastery library of St. Athanasius near Thessalonica, associates the Easter egg tradition with Mary Magdalene. In a prayer of blessing for the Easter eggs, the head of the monastery says, "Thus have we received from the holy Fathers, who preserved this custom from the very time of the holy Apostles. Therefore the holy Equal of the Apostles, Mary Magdalene, first showed believers the example of this joyful offering."[76]

Whether this tradition is true or not, red Easter eggs appropriately announce what Mary Magdalene witnessed and proclaimed. The red-colored egg symbolizes the blood of Jesus shed for us on the cross. The shell symbolizes the sealed tomb after Jesus' burial, whereas cracking the egg symbolizes his resurrection from the dead. Christians around the world, particularly Eastern Christians, maintain this tradition of Easter eggs as a joyful symbol of faith and hope. Once again Mary's leadership among those in authority and her capacity to share the Good News offers a message of hope. She is a testimony of how grace transforms a person into a passionate disciple of Jesus. In the spirit of St. Paul's zealous profession, the love of Christ compelled her.

Mary Magdalene with red egg in her hand[77]

## TO EPHESUS: THE ORTHODOX TRADITION

The Orthodox tradition also claims that Mary Magdalene eventually made her way to Ephesus. There are variations of the story. One claims that after some years of evangelizing work in Rome, she moved to Ephesus. There she accompanied the Apostle John and the Mother of Jesus. The tradition claims that Mary Magdalene was buried there.

Another tradition claims that she accompanied John the Evangelist and Mary, the mother of Jesus, to Ephesus within five years of Jesus' resurrection. Around 1900, Fr. Eugène Poulin went in search of the Virgin Mary's house, following descriptions of Anne Catherine Emmerich's private revelations. He found ruins near Ephesus on the "Hill of Nightingales." The fifth or sixth-century ruins of a house has a first-century foundation. Investigating further, he discovered that the locals had, for generations, commemorated the spot as the house of the Virgin Mary. They also pointed out the place identified as the tomb of Mary Magdalene.

The House of Ephesus

## BURIAL AND RELICS

Various stories reference Mary Magdalene's burial. The Ephesus tradition states that Mary Magdalene's remains were transferred in the ninth century to Constantinople, and placed in the monastery Church of Saint Lazarus. Later, in the era of the Crusader campaigns, they were transferred to Rome and placed under the altar of the Lateran Basilica. This latter piece of data corresponds to the French tradition of her relics being for a time in the Lateran Basilica in Rome.

The French tradition claims that her friend Maximin, the first bishop of Aix, France, buried her in France. The tradition continues, stating that in the year 710, under the reign of a pious King of the Franks and in anticipation of the Saracen invasion, her body was secretly moved from an alabaster tomb to a more hidden marble tomb in the current-day town of Saint-Maximin-la-Sainte-Baume. In 1279, Charles II, King of Naples and Count of Provence, initiated an excavation in the crypt of a small church in Maximim. They found her sarcophagus with a papyrus inside, recounting the details of the transfer of her body in 710. Upon opening the sarcophagus, a sweet smell emanated from within. Excavators also found a wax-covered wood tablet stating in Latin, "Here lies the body of the Blessed Mary Magdalene." The origin of the tablet dates between the first and fourth centuries. The skeleton was missing both her lower jaw and lower leg bones.

It is believed that at some point in history, before 710, her jaw bone was removed and sent to Rome where it remained in the St. John Lateran Basilica, built in the fourth century. To celebrate the discovery of her body, King Charles II commissioned the building of a massive Gothic cathedral in 1295 in Saint Maximin, France. On April 6, 1295, Pope Boniface VIII gave his blessing for the church, returned the jaw bone to reunite it with the rest of the skeletal finds, and placed the Dominican priestly order in charge of the cathedral. To this day, the Dominicans have a special devotion to Mary Magdalene, and the place remains a pilgrim site for those looking to Mary Magdalene for friendly intercession. It is a common practice of the Catholic Church to make relics of the bones or clothing of a saintly person, putting these on display for veneration. The Catholic Church understands that these saints are friends in heaven, "a great cloud of witnesses" (Heb 12:1) who continue to intercede for us. This display of honoring the saints recalls the marvels God has worked in them and through them by His grace and their cooperation.

## FRANCE: THE GOLDEN LEGEND[78]

Pilgrimage to the town of Saint-Maximin-la-Sainte-Baume is rooted in a historical tradition that goes back to a popular Middle Age work called *The Golden Legend*. Mary Magdalene's story is one of many biographies written by Jacobus de Voragine, Archbishop of Genoa, starting around 1260. Jacobus pulled from sources such as Flavius Josephus and Hegesippus, a Father of Church history whose many works have been lost.[79] Mary Magdalene's reputation of fidelity to Jesus and of evangelizing leaders shines through this tradition as well.

Scenes from the Life of Mary Magdalene by Giotto di Bondone

Jacobus wrote his account in the context of the Middle Ages. It was a time of kings, princes, and castles. Within the Church, there was a strong sense of the need for conversion, repentance, and penitence. Mary, portrayed as the sister of Lazarus and Martha, took care of their castle in Magdala. Martha took care of the Bethany house. Mary Magdalene had the reputation of a sinner who converted. She was the repentant woman who anointed Jesus' feet with her tears and precious ointments in Simon the Leper's house in Bethany (Luke 7:36-38). Jesus showed her great love by expelling her seven demons (Mark 16:9) and raising her brother, Lazarus, from the dead (John 11:38-44). Jacobus noted her as the one who chose the better part (Luke 10:42). She performed penance, was the first to be at the feet of Jesus, both when he preached and died on the cross, and she remained at the tomb when others left. Jacobus wrote of Mary's conversion:

❝One day Mary Magdalene heard Jesus preaching from afar in the town of Bethany, and was moved to tears. This incredible experience immediately altered her life forever. She began waiting in the distance just to see him again and to listen to him talk to the people of Bethany. Her heavy heart overflowed with tears of bitterness at the same time as tears of joy, for she had finally discovered true *Love*.[80]

Jacobus's account of the rest of her life paints a picture of her evangelizing zeal and passionate love for Jesus. Peter placed Mary Magdalene under the care of Maximim, one of the seventy-two disciples. About fourteen years after Jesus' crucifixion, a group of Christians was cast into the sea and left to drown as punishment for preaching the word of God. Miraculously they arrived safely in a Roman-occupied city of southern France. Today it is known as Saintes-Maries-de-la-Mer. When Mary saw people worshipping at pagan temples, she began to preach about faith in Jesus. Her beauty, eloquence, and reason amazed many. She even convinced the prince of the province to stop sacrificing to idol gods. She interceded for the prince's wife who miraculously conceived after many barren years. Eventually she retreated into the local hillside, making a hermitage of a cave. It is there that she spent thirty more years of life in solitude and contemplation. Saint Maximim, who eventually became a bishop, attended to her spiritually during that time. During her contemplative period, she offered her life in a spirit of penance for the sins and conversion of others.

Jacobus' panegyric offers readers a model of virtue. The Mary Magdalene of this tradition resembles qualities that could be assumed from reading the Canonical Gospels. 1) She announces her faith in Jesus with an evangelizing spirit. 2) She is influential among leaders, in this case, among civic leaders who had the power to destroy the pagan temples and to help convert the entire town to Christianity. 3) Her spirit of seeking Jesus, which we see in the garden on the day of his resurrection, is played out in this tradition through a spirit of prayerful contemplation. 4) Finally, her transformed life, from *seven demons* to *faithful disciple*, continues through a spirit of penitence, common to medieval spirituality.

## ANOTHER MARY, MARY OF EGYPT[81]

The tradition of Mary's spending thirty years in contemplative and reclusive penitence in a cave of France resembles another Mary, Mary of Egypt, who died around 522 AD. Some speculate that the French tradition morphed out of the tale of Mary of Egypt. Saint Sophronius, a seventh-century Patriarch of Jerusalem, wrote down the story as a dialogue between the holy Abbot Zosimas and Mary of Egypt. Upon Zosimas's meeting Mary in the desert, Mary gave an account of her life of promiscuity.

She recounts that she indulged for many years in order "to have lovers who would satisfy her passions." Seeing a large band of people preparing to set sail from Egypt to Jerusalem for the Exaltation of the Precious and Life-giving Cross, she seduced the sailors to receive passageway. When she reached Jerusalem, she saw everyone attempting to enter the Holy Sepulcher for the exaltation of the Holy Cross. She tried to push her way through the crowd, but a mysterious force would not permit her to enter. After several attempts, she fell exhausted, and it began to dawn on her why she could not enter. She recounts, "The word of salvation gently touched the eyes of my heart and revealed to me that it was my unclean life which barred the entrance to me. I began to weep and lament and beat my breast, and to sigh from the depths of my heart."

Giotto's Zosimas giving Mary his cloak[82]

After repenting, she was able to enter. She saw the life-giving cross, the mysteries of God and how the Lord accepts repentance. Transformed from this moment on, she fled Jerusalem towards the Jordan River where she crossed and spent forty-seven years struggling against her passions, in prayerful repentance, and gained the wisdom of God's revelation without reading any scripture. Zosimas was the first to come upon her after all those years. He was very impressed with her wisdom, austerity, and spirit of penitence. Upon her death, Zosimas buried her.

Mary of Egypt and the tradition of Mary of Magdala in France have various similarities to each other. Those similarities also resonate with characteristics of other historical traditions. Her attainment of divine knowledge and wisdom reflects the previous Gnostic tradition. Her state of being a repentant sinner is present in early Church writings. And Mary of Egypt and Mary of Magdala coincide in their contemplative, reclusive nature. The question remains: Are these mere coincidences and commonalities or was there a merging of stories of these two separate women?

## HELPING OR HINDERING AUTHENTIC SPIRITUAL GROWTH

The ensemble of historical traditions, while seemingly contradictory, offer mosaic pieces of the possible personality of Mary Magdalene. Some of them particularly resonate with aspects of the Canonical Gospels: Her life transformation, her fidelity as a disciple, and her passionate love for Jesus that spurs her on to give witness to him. The pilgrimages and visits to Ephesus and southern France, in remembrance of Mary Magdalene, give witness to her continual influence. Two thousand years ago, Jesus had his eyes on her as a chosen messenger. That appointed task continues today as she inspires hope of a deep encounter with Jesus. She is still a chosen messenger who points the way to conversion of heart, passionate love for Jesus, and deeper discipleship. She remains human in her saintly state, not embodying divine femininity, but with the privilege of being in the presence of the Risen Lord in his glory. From this point of view, disciples of Jesus can befriend Mary Magdalene. Both interior transformations and exterior miracles have been attributed to her intercession through the centuries. In a spirit of the communion of saints, Christians call upon her to pray for them and to present their intentions to the Lord.

The challenge today is for Christians to maintain a healthy admiration without being drawn in by the syncretistic pull to intermingle popular Christian devotion with cultic-pagan practices. Christians must discern and purify these devotions so that they are truly experiences leading to authentic spiritual growth in the life of Christ. Mary has become a model for femininity at its best, and represents a woman, who, like all saints, has attained a certain "divinization." But rather than seeing Mary Magdalene as a goddess herself, admirers are invited to marvel at the work of grace within her. Her appeal is her genuine humanity, like clay in the potter's hands. She was justified and sanctified through her free acceptance of conversion and her life of following Jesus. After Pentecost, she would have discovered the power of the Holy Spirit in her life. As St. Athanasius said, "[God] gave himself to us through his Spirit. By the participation of the Spirit, we become communicants in the divine nature. (...) For this reason, those in whom the Spirit dwells are divinized."[83] Saint Peter also referred to the process of conversion and spiritual growth and our "divinization," or participation in the divine nature.

> His divine power has given us everything we need for a godly life through our knowledge of him who called us by his glory and goodness. Through these he has given us his very great and precious promises, so that through them you may participate in the divine nature, having escaped the corruption in the world caused by evil desires. For this very reason, make every effort to add to your faith goodness; and to goodness, knowledge; and to knowledge, self-control; and to self-control, perseverance; and to perseverance, godliness; and to godliness, mutual affection; and to mutual affection, love. For, if you possess these qualities in increasing measure, they will keep you from being ineffective and unproductive in your knowledge of our Lord Jesus Christ.
>
> —I Peter 1:3-8

The process of sanctification lasts a lifetime and is a mystery of "dialogue" between God's grace and human freedom. This process does not entail a change in our human nature to a divine nature, but rather a participation in God's very life. God remains God and we remain human, without any annihilation of human personality or change in our status as an image of God. The rough diamond becomes polished, and the wet shapeless clay becomes molded. Ultimately, the process of spiritual growth is a way to glorify God. The glory of God is the human person full of God's grace and alive in the Spirit.[84] Mary Magdalene would surely like to voice her opinion in this regard, saying, "I stand before you as a mere mortal, yet redeemed and sanctified by my God. Look to Him who has been pierced for your transgressions. To think of me is to see the marvels the Lord can do with you too if you but let him be the One Lord of your life."

## MARY MAGDALENE IN THE TRADITION OF ART: LIFE LESSONS FOR EVERY CENTURY

The art of Mary Magdalene through the centuries reflects how her figure continues to convey spiritual truths. A full survey of Mary Magdalene in art is not the scope of this section, but a glimpse into a few works should suffice to see the rich theological and spiritual reflection she offers every age. Interpretations of her character, associations with historical events and a strengthening devotion eventually brought her into the spotlight as a solitary figure. Before the Middle Ages, however, she has her place within a broader catechesis, like the Paschal mystery scenes of the crucifixion and resurrection of Jesus in the sixth-century illumination from the Rabbula Gospels.[85] She is but one figure among many weeping women at the cross, the women at the empty tomb and the witnesses of Jesus' appearance after his resurrection. Finally, in the late Middle Ages she begins to be singled out.

The illumination from the Rabbula Gospels; Mary Magdalene at the crucifixion and the resurrection is one among several other women present. *(public domain)*

## SYMBOLS ASSOCIATED WITH MARY MAGDALENE

Religious themes dominated the Proto-Renaissance and early Renaissance periods from the fourteenth to sixteenth centuries. Mary Magdalene appears as the grief-stricken woman or the penitent prostitute in several works of prominent European artists of those days. What did Mary Magdalene offer Christians of that era?

The Black Death consumed one-third of Western Europe's population. Identifying with a grief-stricken Mary Magdalene, who witnessed her beloved's crucifixion and death, must have brought consolation to those enduring the tantamount loss of loved ones. The daily encounter with death brought themes like eternity, salvation, conversion, and repentance to the forefront of people's minds. Perhaps Mary Magdalene, as a repentant sinner, spoke to the hearts of many in those days.

Fra Angelico's *Crucifixion* (1441)[86]

The image of Mary Magdalene as a penitent prostitute with long flowing hair also reflects an association with Luke's account of the unnamed sinner who wiped Jesus' feet with her hair. From the fourteenth to the sixteenth century, courtesans would often dye their hair blond.[87] Whether she was painted as a blond or redhead, flowing hair, rather than braided hair as seen in the earlier Jewish tradition, alluded to her former reputation as a woman of ill-repute.

Even though the paintings reflect a post-conversion Mary Magdalene, the artists display her reputation with symbolism. For example, Fra Angelico's painting of 1441 portrays the crucifixion with Mary Magdalene clinging to the cross below Jesus' feet. She is the only one painted with an exposed head of hair. Her uncovered head reveals blond hair flowing down her back.

Mary Magdalene's partial nudity reflects the Greco-Roman influence that is revived in Renaissance art, portraying realism and the beauty of the body. Titian (1490-1576), an Italian Renaissance artist, painted two Penitent Mary Magdalenes, one in the 1530s and another in the 1560s. Both present Mary with long blondish to light red hair, an ointment jar at her side, and a gaze that penetrates the heavens with a look of longing, while her right hand covers her heart. In his first painting, she appears with her breasts fully exposed. In the second painting, Titian covered her breasts slightly and painted a skull and book in her lap. El Greco's depiction in his 1577 painting reveals similar features: a look of longing mingled with sorrow, flowing red hair, her breast exposed as she is scantily dressed, an ointment jar at her side and a skull and book in her lap. His later 1580 painting paints her more modestly and with blondish hair.

Guido Reni painted four Mary Magdalenes in the early 17th century, all similar with her contemplative ecstatic glances towards the heavens, her long flowing reddish-blond hair, and a loose-fitting dress. However, in each one of the four paintings, something unique stands out: her hand is on a skull as angels hover in the heavens; two hands are over her heart as she is in prayerful ecstasy; her gaze is lovingly fixed upon a crucifix; and one hand is holding an ointment jar.

*(above)* Titian's *Penitent St. Mary Magdalene* (1560 version)[88];
*(below)* El Greco (1577 version)[89]

Guido Reni's *St. Mary Magdalene* (1632 version)[90]

## INTERPRETING SYMBOLISM TO UNVEIL THE MYSTERY

While all of these depictions are a reflection of her life after her conversion, their artistic rendition alludes to her assumed promiscuous past, her present state of fidelity to Jesus, and her longing for a future yet to be attained. The symbols strikingly speak of the drama of human redemption: past, present, and future. While artworks reflect particular cultural and historical contexts, rich themes speak to a universal and perennial audience through their symbolism.

One theme is the *restoration of original nakedness*. Mary Magdalene's flowing hair and partial nudity recall the time in the garden when Adam and Eve walked naked and without shame. Her nudity recalls the nuptial meaning of bodily existence. It speaks of the human person's vocation to loving communion with God and others. It symbolizes her acceptance of Jesus' redemption through a spirit of faith and repentance. Jesus "restores" her original nakedness in a new and unique way. Her freedom can now be used to participate in Jesus' redemptive work rather than against it.

The application of the redemptive grace that Jesus has won for all and the restoration of humanity's original state is a journey through the cross. Mary's contemplation of the cross speaks of this. It is a journey completed by the grace of God, yet it requires acceptance and receptiveness. The process requires a *death to self*. The vessel of myrrh, symbolizing her willingness to anoint Jesus' dead body, represents Mary's death to sin. It is an invitation to die to the idols of life, particularly self-idolatry that festers in selfishness.

The skull places the viewer face to face with the *fugacity of life* and invites all to an *examination of conscience*. The skull is evidence of mortality, the end of all human life, for saints and sinners alike. Death is inevitable. Keeping a skull in view as a reminder of one's eventual death was an age-old practice in monasteries. And cemeteries were often at the center of the cloister. These practices provoke a glimpse into the truth of one's self before God, thus evoking a *spirit of repentance*. George de La Tour depicts this well in his two paintings of the Repentant Mary Magdalene. Rather than appearing with deep grief, she gently rests one hand on the skull. She prayerfully and reflectively stares into a mirror. In his first rendition (1630), Mary sees the skull reflected back to her. It recalls Ecclesiastes 1:2, "Vanity of vanities; all is vanity." In his later rendition (1643), a lit candle appears in the mirror, much like the light of God's life that shines out from the eyes of one living in the truth.

George de la Tour's *The Repenting Magdalene*[91]
1630 version *(above)*; 1643 version *(below)*

Another theme present when interpreting Mary Magdalene paintings is *the restless heart's longing for fulfillment* and its *taste of eternity* in prayer. Mary's expression of longing and sometimes ecstatic glance towards the heavens is a sign of the journeying soul who has yet to arrive at the finish line, the eternal paradise in which God will be all in all (1 Cor 15:28).

The empty jar standing in front of the skull, seen in El Greco's 1580 painting, represents her response to being set free. Her love is poured out upon the Lord in this life. She continues to give all of herself and awaits the final consummation of union with her Beloved. Contemplative prayer enkindles her longing for the Lord, where God "gifts" a foretaste of eternity to those who sincerely seek him.

El Greco (1580)[92]

Mary Magdalene's *solidarity with sufferers* caught the attention of many at the beginning of the nineteenth century. The Neo-classical French sculptor Antonio Canova portrayed Mary Magdalene's quiet and gentle sorrow. His sculpture was created and displayed publicly on the cusp of the 1789 French Revolution and 1801 Concordat. The French Revolution sought to de-Christianize the state. The Concordat was an agreement between Napoleon and the Pope that sought to restore some of the Catholic Church's status. In the midst of this power play, Mary Magdalene stood as a witness once again. Under Napoleon's revolution, millions lost their lives. She offered a consoling figure with whom many could identify. In Canova's 1796 marble statute, Mary Magdalene silently grieves. Her slouched shoulders lean forward as her head bows towards her chest. Her hands openly lie on her lap as though receptive in prayer and receiving the consolation of peace in the midst of suffering. A skull sits near her left knee, and a tear slides down her face. In some portraits of the sculpture, a simple bronze cross sits in her hands, symbolizing her union with the cross of Christ.

Antonio Canova (1796)[93]

John Collier offers contemporary twenty-first-century hearts another picture of solidarity. His statue stands at Ground Zero's Catholic memorial (Manhattan, New York). As the first witness to the horrors of the crucifixion, Mary Magdalene's compassionate gaze stands in solidarity with the living witnesses of those who died in the terrorist attack of 9/11.

Her appearance is beautiful but sober in her sorrow. Her clothing is modest; she is not in a state of undress. Breaking from previous traditions, Collier portrays her hair beyond shoulder-length but not remarkably long. His use of Mary carrying spice jars is faithful to the Gospel account. She is a myrrh-bearer on her way to Jesus' tomb, not necessarily the "penitent woman with the alabaster jar." The sense of movement transmitted by Collier's Mary Magdalene reflects her active engagement with the event at hand. He sculpts her in motion, looking outward and upward. She approaches the scene with her hands full, carrying two jars. Her presence is like an icon of compassionate love. She comes as a bearer of the Good News. She offers hope amidst sorrow, reminding us that we can look beyond suffering and death to the resurrection.

John Collier's *Mary Magdalene at Ground Zero*[94]

# PART IV: THE LIFE-TRANSFORMING ENCOUNTER
*Insights from Twenty-First Century Ancient Magdala*

What is the relevance of Mary Magdalene in the twenty-first century? In a time when our culture places freedom as the ultimate value, we need authentic role models who show us the way to true freedom, a freedom rooted in humility as we recognize our deep need for redemption. We need models that inspire conversion, from the self-centeredness that dominates the heart and breaks down relationships, to a selflessness that fosters life and true communion among peoples. We need models that prove to us the beauty of magnanimity, those who have taken up the torch to do great things for God, despite their shortcomings and apparent failures. Mary Magdalene is precisely that. She is one among many models. So many faithful disciples of Jesus have fought the good fight and finished the race. Many were hidden from the public spotlight, whereas others received the title of "saint" in the public eye and through the affirmation of their witness of holiness. Each one of them, chosen and touched by God, allowed him to work wonders within and through them.

God comes into the lives of people, not abstractly, but in a real, concrete way. The pinnacle of that coming was the incarnation, when the *Word of God-made-flesh* dwelt among us. God continues his presence among us, in and through the Holy Spirit. The history of the saints reveals the creativity of the Holy Spirit at work. Real transformations reveal how God enters the lives of his people in a concrete place and period and addresses the very specific circumstances that they face. These testimonies are not meant to be isolated and merely private events, but work to build up the body of Christ, the Church. The saints become salt and light in the world, "incarnate realities" of God's saving presence and action in the continued drama of salvation history. They become icons that point the way to authentic living, living according to a God-given dignity and purpose. The Holy Land, and places like Magdala, become invitations to a deeper Christian living by reminding us of the people who walked into the light, and then became a beacon for others to follow. Mary Magdalene remains a light for us today. And what better place to meet her than in Ancient Magdala!

## THE STONES CRY OUT

As Jesus descended the Mount of Olives towards the Holy City of Jerusalem, a multitude of followers rejoiced and praised God for all the wonders they had seen. Some people rebuked Jesus, demanding that they stop. He answered, "I tell you, if they keep quiet, the stones will cry out" (Luke 19:37-40). In Ancient Magdala, the stones cry out as a witness to the drama of life and the hope of redemption. The stones take us back to a past where Jesus walked among the people, teaching, healing, expelling demons, and offering his redemptive love to all who showed a glimmer of openness. They remind us of the universal plight of humankind throughout the ages. While the "dead" stones remind us of a living past, it is the living stones, people from Mary Magdalene to the present day, who have kept hope alive by proclaiming a Gospel of redemption and reconciliation.

Jesus told his disciples, "Go out to the entire world and tell the Good News" (Mt 16:15). Today, in Magdala, people from the four corners of the earth visit and remember God's merciful love. But this is not exclusive to Magdala. It is the case for much of the Holy Land. The holy sites are special places where the kerygma plants itself in the minds and hearts of pilgrims. Despite the plethora of Christian denominations that now exist, they share one kerygma, the central apostolic proclamation that we are saved by grace through faith in Jesus Christ overflowing in love. And so the holy sites become a "fifth Gospel" where a composition of place entices the Gospel imagination. Through contemplating the mysteries of faith in the Land where they historically took place, God's grace unlocks the heart for Jesus to enter and the Holy Spirit gives his gifts in the present.

Holy sites stimulate people on their faith journey: from searchers uncertain of what to believe, to cradle Christians who have yet to experience a profound encounter with the Lord, to those who have been tested in fire and continue to surrender their lives as disciples of Jesus. Through the biblical sites, the Holy Spirit enkindles faith and forges apostles. From Mary Magdalene to the present-day pilgrims, the encounter with God's goodness and merciful love is personal. While Mary's life was unique and her role as the first recorded witness cannot be repeated, much of her experience can be our own. In Ancient Magdala, we are invited to enter into the mystery of God's love.

# ENTERING INTO THE MYSTERY

## *A COMPOSITION OF PLACE: ENCOUNTERS IN MAGDALA'S MARKETPLACE AND SYNAGOGUE*

On the far north side of town, an east-west road lies between the synagogue and marketplace and leads down to the port. These ruins offer a composition of place for Jesus' preaching and healing ministry, as well as Mary Magdalene's observance of Jesus' charismatic personality. Even before she begins to follow Jesus through Galilee (Lk 24:6), she was likely a curious bystander as he entered the synagogue and marketplace. Imagine what she may have seen as she walked about Ancient Magdala.

Jesus has many run-ins with the Pharisees in the Galilee region. No one has ruled out the possibility that Pharisees lived in Magdala. Mary witnesses Jesus' interactions with them. He warns them, "Woe to you Pharisees because you love the front seats in the *synagogues* and the greetings in the *marketplaces*!" (Luke 11:43, emphasis added). Jesus appears to be very observant of their behavior. He sees beyond the façade. Mary senses that he also sees through her façade. In the midst of the cultural and religious trends of her time, Jesus is very bold and, at times, counter-cultural. His capacity to profoundly see into the heart of each person piqued her curiosity.

The road between the synagogue and marketplace

Mary observes Jesus in the marketplace as the Pharisees approach him

As Jesus walks the shores of the Sea of Galilee and calls his first disciples, she hears him proclaiming the Good News, "The time has come. The Kingdom of God has come near. Repent and believe the Good News!" (Mk 1:14-15). These words struck a chord, provoking a deeper examination of conscience about her life circumstances and choices. She draws near to hear more of his preaching. She listens to him as he teaches in the synagogues. Luke gives us an account of his visit to the synagogues of Galilee, particularly Nazareth. Imagine if a similar event took place in Magdala's synagogue and Mary had been there.

❝ ... on the Sabbath day he went into the synagogue, as was his custom. He stood up to read, and the scroll of the prophet Isaiah was handed to him. Unrolling it, he found the place where it is written:

> "The Spirit of the Lord is upon me,
> because he has anointed me
> to proclaim good news to the poor.
> He has sent me to proclaim freedom for the prisoners
> and recovery of sight for the blind,
> to set the oppressed free,
> to proclaim the year of the Lord's favor."

Then he rolled up the scroll, gave it back to the attendant and sat down. The eyes of everyone in the synagogue were fastened on him. He began by saying to them, "Today this scripture is fulfilled in your hearing."

—Luke 4:16-21

The eyes of Mary Magdalene fix on Jesus; her ears are attentive to his voice. As she listens to him, hope abounds in her heart. She identifies with his words. She knows what it feels like to be a prisoner, blind, oppressed. She longs for freedom and recovery from her present condition. Not only is her curiosity piqued, but an attraction forms. She is on the alert for his presence. She begins to seek him out and witnesses his many miracles. The Gospels give the impression that Jesus cured a large number in the region surrounding Magdala.

❝ When they had crossed over, they landed at Gennesaret and anchored there. As soon as they got out of the boat, people recognized Jesus. They ran throughout that whole region and carried the sick on mats to wherever they heard he was. And wherever he went—into villages, towns or countryside—

IC XC, used at the sides of the halo, is a traditional abbreviation
of the Greek words for Jesus Christ.

they placed the sick in the marketplaces. They begged him to let them touch even the edge of his cloak, and all who touched it were healed.

—Mark 6:53-56

Perhaps she was familiar with Malachi's prophecy, "For those who revere my name, the sun of righteousness will rise with healing in his wings" (Malachi 4:2). Perhaps Mary understood the fulfilment of this prophecy as many touched the "wings," or corner, of Jesus' prayer garment and were healed.[95] She begins to entertain the thought of meeting Jesus face to face. She hopes that she too could be healed, but she wonders if his power was great enough to liberate her from her present situation. She continues to search for him, accompanying the crowd that follows him, perhaps even to Capernaum.

Magdala is a two-hour walk from Capernaum. Mark gives an account of Jesus healing a man with an unclean spirit in the synagogue and Jesus' fame increases with the healing of Simon Peter's mother-in-law. The whole city brings the sick to him, hoping for a miracle. The next morning he goes out to a deserted place to pray, but his disciples find him and report that many are still looking for him. He tells them, "'Let us go on to the next towns, that I may preach there also, for that is why I came out.' And he went throughout all Galilee, preaching in their synagogues and casting out demons" (Mk 1:38-39).

The gospels do not give an account of Jesus in Magdala, but it is highly possible considering the geographical location and the fact that Jesus went about teaching in the synagogues of Galilee (Mk 1:39). Nor is it known if women were in the synagogue there. We see the possibility, however, in Luke 13:10-17.

On a Sabbath, Jesus was teaching in one of the synagogues, and a woman was there who had been crippled by a spirit for eighteen years. She was bent over and could not straighten up at all. When Jesus saw her, he called her forward and said to her, "Woman, you are set free from your infirmity." Then he put his hands on her, and immediately she straightened up and praised God.

Indignant because Jesus had healed on the Sabbath, the synagogue leader said to the people, "There are six days for work. So come and be healed on those days, not on the Sabbath."

The Lord answered him, "You hypocrites! Doesn't each of you on the Sabbath untie your ox or donkey from the stall and lead it out to give it water? Then should not this woman, a daughter of Abraham, whom Satan has kept bound for eighteen long years, be set free on the Sabbath day from what bound her?"

When he said this, all his opponents were humiliated, but the people were delighted with all the wonderful things he was doing.

—Luke 13:10-17

The tension was building between Jesus and his critics. And yet, more and more people were flocking to him to be healed. By now, Mary Magdalene's curiosity has turned to admiration and awe. She senses the authenticity of his care for each person. A higher law of genuine acceptance and mercy dominates his criteria for action. He heals many people precisely on the day of rest, revealing his intention and power to complete God's creative action and restore wholeness to those who approach him with faith and trust. And he acts despite the criticism from local authorities and religious leaders. She witnesses his genuine care and boldness again and again.

Again he entered the synagogue, and a man was there with a withered hand. And they watched Jesus, to see whether he would heal him on the Sabbath so that they might accuse him. And he said to the man with the withered hand, "Come here." And he said to them, "Is it lawful on the Sabbath to do good or to do harm, to save a life or to kill?" But they were silent. And he looked around at them with anger, grieved at their hardness of heart, and said to the man, "Stretch out your hand." He stretched it out, and his hand was restored.

The Pharisees went out and immediately held counsel with the Herodians against him, how to destroy him.

—Mark 3:1-6

Mark alludes to Pharisees and Herodians as Jesus' opponents. But he also mentions those who were "delighted with the wonderful things he was doing" (Lk 13:17). Mary Magdalene is among them. In Jesus, she finds an answer to the cultural, moral, and religious inconsistencies and perplexities in her surroundings as well as in her very person. After witnessing so many healings and liberations, she feels a spark of determination. She boldly desires to open

Jesus heals the crippled woman

her heart to Jesus. When she eventually meets him face to face, a powerful transformation overtakes her. Of this the Gospels only allude, calling her the Magdalene, from whom seven demons were expelled (Lk 8:2). It is unknown if the drama of Mary's deliverance took place in Magdala, but the synagogue offers a visual for the Gospel imagination. From this point on, her love for and fidelity to Jesus will be tested and strengthened.

## CONTEMPLATING THE POWER OF AN ENCOUNTER AND WITNESS

When it comes to the marvelous encounter between the risen Jesus and Mary, John seemed to have some deeper insights than some of his fellow evangelists. A prior powerful encounter with Jesus, in which he cast out her seven demons, transformed Mary into a faithful follower. She proves her devotion at the foot of the cross. Now her being for Jesus is rewarded as she encounters him in his resurrected presence. John's account in the garden recounts similar features to the synoptic evangelists, yet the drama unfolds with echoes of the Song of Songs: a lover searches for her beloved and, at last, finds him. Her joyous proclamation, "I have seen the Lord!" (Jn 20:18), is the climax of initial confusion and bewilderment that turns to joy, awe, and a heart-moving encounter.

Starting at the beginning of John's resurrection account, Mary Magdalene's instincts as an apostle move her to instigate John and Peter's search for Jesus. Luke alludes to the fact that Jesus also appears to Peter that same day (Lk 24:34). But his time has not yet come for that encounter. Perplexed, Peter and John then "went back to where they were staying" (Jn. 20:10). "They still did not understand from Scriptures that Jesus had to rise from the dead" (Jn. 20:9). But Mary remains in the garden.

Let us go to the garden with Mary. She weeps. As she weeps, she sees two angels who ask her why she is crying. She turns around, and Jesus is before her. Through tear-filled eyes and due to Jesus' resurrected appearance, she mistakes him for the gardener. Certainly, he knows perfectly well that Mary is searching for him, yet he asks, "Woman, why are you crying? Who is it you are looking for?" (Jn. 20:15). As though he longs to see the expression of her love, he elicits her response. She mistakes him for the gardener until suddenly she hears her name. "Mary." What makes her finally recognize Jesus? It is the tenderness and familiarity of his voice. It suddenly breaks through her grieved reverie, and she cries out "Rabboni!" He is her teacher, her master, her guide. She has found the one for whom she searched. John doesn't describe the scene in detail, but it is enough to hear Jesus commanding her, "Do not hold on to me," to get the picture. She launches herself forward to embrace the One for whom her heart longed.

Jesus does not permit her to remain there long, clinging to him. He sends her away with the Good News rooted deeply within. Her mission is to announce the Good News to the foundation stones of his Church (Rev. 21:14). She is not moved by mere obedience, but by loving compulsion. She could exclaim as St. Paul did several years later, "Christ's love compels us because we are convinced that one died for all…" (2 Cor. 5:14).

The disciples of Emmaus also receive the honor of walking with and speaking with Jesus during that Sunday of his resurrection. As he broke the bread they recognized him. After he disappeared, they "got up and returned at once to Jerusalem. There they found the Eleven and those with them, assembled together and saying, 'It is true! The Lord has risen and has appeared to Simon'" (Lk. 24: 33-34). From the beginning of the day to the end of the day, Jesus made himself known to many. But the first witness was a woman, Mary Magdalene.

The honor bestowed on her speaks of the trust Jesus has for a woman whose passionate love drives her to share the Good News at the cost of ridicule and disbelief. Being an apostle, and in her case, the Apostle to the Apostles, must have been a challenging role. The Kingdom of God is not in its perfect, visible form here on earth, and the early Church suffered challenges inside and out. Among those who animated the others to keep the faith was Mary Magdalene, living alongside many other disciples, and helping to build a community of believers with courage, passion, and love.

Now, Mary Magdalene becomes a model for Christians who desire to more fully participate in Jesus' priestly, prophetic, and kingly mission. A priestly mission implies self-sacrifice and the daily uniting of sufferings "at the foot of the cross" to the sacrifice of Jesus. A prophetic mission is lived out by being a witness and bearer of the Good News. A kingly mission is fulfilled as Jesus reigns central in our heart. Like Mary Magdalene, we are called to participate in the redemptive mission of Jesus. This participation is a path by which we discover our dignity, learn to use our freedom authentically, and become salt and light in the world.

## THE INVITATION TO BE SALT & LIGHT

God never imposes himself, but always invites. Human persons, made in God's image, are free to accept or reject God's invitation to a full and authentic living of their dignity. When they use their freedom to serve God, to love neighbor and to live the Gospel message even to the point of death of self in the physical or spiritual realm, they become salt and light for the world. They stand witness to the possibilities in our own lives. The saints are salt that flavors the Christian journey and beacons to signal the way. While the Holy Spirit acts in and through the saints, the light "needs oil," the part each person puts as they freely and lovingly respond to God's initiative. Jesus himself reveals the importance of that light shining through good works.

> You are light for the world. A city built on a hill-top cannot be hidden. No one lights a lamp to put it under a tub; they put it on the lamp-stand where it shines for everyone in the house. In the same way, your light must shine in people's sight, so that, seeing your good works, they may give praise to your Father in heaven.
>
> —Mt. 5:14-16

The light that shines forth from holy people has a far-reaching scope. It is no wonder that people like Mary Magdalene, Mother Teresa, Francis of Assisi, and holy men and women through the centuries have become so appealing. The beauty of humanity redeemed attracts believers and non-believers alike. Thus, admiration of saints is not exclusive to Christians. That is why they sometimes become "fads" in a particular period. It seems that Mary Magdalene has become this today.

## MARY MAGDALENE FOR THE SECULAR WORLD

In the present-day site of ancient Magdala where Jews, Christians, atheists, and non-professed searchers come daily, Mary Magdalene speaks to all. While the Christian traditions are theologically rich in their reflections on Mary Magdalene, she offers food for thought to even the secular mind and heart. Here are a few "takeaways" with which even non-believers can identify.

Mary Magdalene is an *Icon of Hope*. While ultimate healing comes from the source of life, namely God, the experience of unconditional love, from a spouse, parent, or friend is, in a sense, healing. Mary Magdalene was healed of something that plagued her. Love healed her. Love heals. Authentic and sincere love is the keystone for recognizing one's dignity and has the power to transform lives. Perhaps we gain light about Mary Magdalene's experience when Jesus sets her free of her bonds.

Mary Magdalene is a *Model of Interior Freedom*. Her character stands out as bold and determined. She was likely so before and after her conversion. Her initial "reckless" freedom transforms into virtuous interior freedom. Freedom is a gift to treasure and care for, not abuse. The end-all-be-all of the human person is not to be free of all inhibitions, but to use one's freedom in conjunction with one's dignity, to live a fully human life of authentic love and self-giving. Mary's passionate love for Jesus reveals her deep interior freedom, evident when she accompanies him in his public life and follows him to the foot of the cross. She breaks from cultural norms to follow Jesus around Galilee, not for the sake of merely expressing her capacity to do as she pleases, but because there is a higher value at stake. She discovers that she is a better person when she is with him. At the foot of the cross, she is not inhibited by human respect or fear of what others think of her. She follows the path of fidelity to the one who truly sought her greatest good. And now she sacrifices herself to return that love. People of all walks of life can recognize the strength of a woman's passionate love, a love that doesn't seek temporal pleasures above all else but collaborates in a far nobler project.

Mary Magdalene is a *Model of Leadership*, particularly for women. Without a doubt, many of the historical traditions portray her as a leader among leaders. But she is also a model for women who feel themselves as second-class citizens or who do not believe in their capacity to influence others. She reminds women to "remain woman," to value their femininity, and to believe that they can play an important role in society with their sincere gift of self. In the twenty-first century, women are leaders within their families, within their workplace, and within ministries. At the same time, women are still fighting against inequality in the workplace where they are being paid less for the same position as men. They are still striving to be respected within their own household, especially in cultures where the education of women is frowned upon. Mary Magdalene reminds women that they can boldly and confidently proclaim a message and forge ahead despite any cultural or institutional injustice. She exemplifies the potential of a woman on fire for a cause.

Through that leadership, Mary Magdalene also becomes a *Voice for the Exploited*, particularly those who are objectified and made to be a sport for others. Contemporary culture sells and consumes human flesh without looking into the eyes of the human person. It sees the human body as a commodity without a voice, feelings, or dignity. Pornography, prostitution, sexual assault and emotional manipulation for personal gain enslave both the offenders and the offended.[96] The human person's ultimate purpose, to love and be loved, is thwarted due to the lies spoken by manipulation, greed, and lust.

While Mary Magdalene's reputation as a prostitute is questionable, she nonetheless has become associated with figures whose life of promiscuity is degrading and makes them an object of someone else's pleasure. Those who have fallen into the trap of prostitution and experienced the chains of exploitation may look to Mary Magdalene to muster up hope for a new beginning. She also could have known the guilt, shame, disgust, and the plethora of emotions and deep wounds that men and women experience when their pleas for justice remain unresolved.[97] If nothing else, she offers a face of solidarity for victims of sexual assault and harassment whose voices go unheard.

Mary Magdalene's life testifies to the *Power of Witness*. In an age that disregarded women's witness, she nonetheless spoke what she saw. Her message brought the truth of a situation to light, and it has resonated through the centuries, revealing the power of testimony. Nonetheless, her timeless influence comes from a Christian reading. The perennial charm of Mary Magdalene is her message of realism and hope. She shows us that in the messiness of life, Jesus met her where she was and offered her a new and better way. No matter where we are in our life, Jesus does the same for us.

## A SPIRITUALITY OF ENCOUNTER & AUTHENTIC FREEDOM

The beauty of the saints is that their influence does not die with their death. Their example attracts us to live a more authentic Christian life. The saints give witness to a lived experience of revelation that sometimes takes the form of a particular spirituality. Spiritualities take shape and emerge through various elements, including a saint's testimony of life, preaching and writings, and future generations' reflections about them. They aid Christians in their journey to a deeper relationship with God. They act as invitations to enter into the dynamics of God's saving action dialoguing with human freedom. Spiritualities are signs that the Holy Spirit speaks and works, perpetually and creatively.

Christian spiritualities are rooted in revelation, a revelation that was completed in Jesus Christ. But the richness of his person is inexhaustible. Therefore, they offer a mere glimpse into the vast mystery of God's incarnate love. While it may sound presumptuous to say that there is an emerging spirituality in Magdala, the dynamic of Mary Magdalene's life journey speaks to countless visitors today. This "spirituality," if we can dare to call it that, invites Christians to:

1. Contemplate the personal and unconditional love of Jesus.
2. Recognize, in humility and realism, the need for redemption.

3.   Hope in God's power to heal, liberate and restore us to wholeness.

4.   Believe in our dignity and call to live authentic freedom.

5.   Ask for fortitude in the face of suffering, aware of the redemptive value of all suffering united to Christ's cross.

6.   Be courageous witnesses of faith in Jesus and proclaim the Good News, especially to those of influence, so as to bring the Good News to a far-reaching scope.

From ancient Magdala, contemporary Christians are invited to reflect upon the mystery of God's personal love and His invitation to deeper discipleship. Mary Magdalene's testimony acts as a springboard. It all starts with an *encounter*. The chapel mosaic, created by Maria Jesús Fernandez de Ortiz, tells the story. Let's look at her mosaic and let it speak to us.

## BACK TO THE GARDEN

The scene portrayed in Magdala's mosaic chapel cannot be found directly in Sacred Scriptures, but it is alluded to in Mark 16:9 and Luke 8:2. Mary is the one from whom Jesus expels seven demons. Beyond that knowledge, the "Gospel imagination" has to kick in. A prayerful contemplation of artistic renditions of Gospel scenes, such as this one, helps viewers enter into a Gospel scene, to "read between the lines," and make personal applications.

Mary Magdalene chapel mosaic in the Duc in Altum church, Magdala

In the mosaic, Mary Magdalene comes face to face with Jesus. It is above all, a transforming encounter with unconditional love. She stands in a garden, reminiscent of the Garden of Eden, yet she is here at the foot of Mount Arbel, in her hometown of Magdala. The image of the garden brings us back to the beginning when man and woman walked freely in the presence of God. They were naked, yet without shame (Gen. 2:25). That is, they were clothed with God's glory and walked freely until succumbing to the temptation to be on equal terms with God.

Seven demons lurk behind her. Six little demons fly off and one large serpent slither down the tree, yet its tail still lingers upon her arm. The serpent represents the first tempter, instrumental in luring Eve and Adam to their first fall from innocence. After the fall, they recognized their new condition and felt ashamed to face God. "I was naked, so I hid" (Gen. 3:10). That was the beginning of the banishment from the garden. But it was not the end of the story.

## A NEW CREATION

Along comes Jesus. His pointed finger captures the attention. It is pointed right at Mary. Is he condemning her? Shaking his finger at her and telling her "naughty, naughty girl!"? On the contrary! Jesus points his finger, not to condemn her, but to set her free. The finger alludes to the possibility of a new beginning. Michelangelo painted a similar finger onto the ceiling of the Sistine Chapel in the Vatican. God the Father creates Adam. In the beginning, God gave new life. In the history of humanity, God continues offering new life again in his Son through his Holy Spirit. Now, in the mosaic, Jesus offers Mary the gift of becoming a new creation.

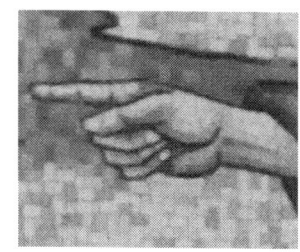

The finger of God

## INITIATION INTO GOD'S KINGDOM

Luke 11:20 also comes into play here. Jesus tells the Pharisees, "But if it is by the finger of God that I drive out demons, then the Kingdom of God has come upon you." The "finger of God" appears in two passages in the Hebrew Bible, Exodus 8:19 & 31:18. In Exodus 8:19, magicians warn Pharaoh that the plagues on Egypt are set upon them by the finger of God. In other words, the power of God is at work. The Egyptians finally admit defeat and allow the Jewish people liberation from slavery under Moses' leadership. The finger of God prefigures "the mighty hand and outstretched arm" of God, who delivers his people through "his Holy Spirit." The Holy Spirit is the power that binds Satan.

Jesus is the New Moses who comes to set all free from the slavery of sin and establish a New Covenant. He overcomes Satan and ushers in the Kingdom of God with his very Person. He establishes the Kingdom through the Holy Spirit. Jesus' words, "Repent for the Kingdom of God is at hand," were likely heard by Mary Magdalene. Her curiosity drew her to him. His words acted as seeds that now begin to blossom in the present. She freely accepts the gift. The moment of liberation takes place. Where death once threatened the soul, life now reigns.

Jesus offers life, symbolized in the mosaic by the blooming flowers surrounding Jesus. Echoes of Isaiah 35: 1-2 ring out:

> ❝The desert and the parched land will be glad;
> the wilderness will rejoice and blossom.
> Like the crocus, it will burst into bloom;
> it will rejoice greatly and shout for joy.

Flowers around Jesus' feet

Jesus not only offers life, he is the life. Mary Magdalene, standing in the Garden with seven demons fleeing out of her, represents a "New Eve" as she receives new life in Christ.

Her face reflects the fruit of this new beginning and the life of the Spirit coming upon her: peace and joy. In the words of St. Paul, "The Kingdom of God is not a matter of eating or drinking, but of justice, peace and the joy that is given by the Holy Spirit" (Romans 14:17). Mary is invited to participate in the Kingdom of God. It is now her task to walk in faith, hope, and love, awaiting the final

Face of Mary Magdalene

The dog growling

consummation of God's Kingdom with persevering confidence. For the moment, in this temporal realm, she will experience the fruit of Jesus' redemption, which is a mere taste of what is to come. Until then, "All creation is groaning in anticipation of the redemption that awaits mankind" (Romans 8:18-25). The dog, growling at the demons, seems to reflect creation awaiting the fullness of God's promise.

## RECOGNIZING BONDAGE

The demons that lurk behind Mary may sound like a child's tale told to teach a lesson, but it throws into relief a human condition and experience. The "demons" that tempt and bind the human person today range from unsatisfied desires for intimacy that lead to addictive behaviors like pornography, to a life afflicted with trauma or abuse, to cultural stigma, prejudices, or self-deprecating thoughts of our worth. Women are especially proficient at this: "I will never be good enough" or "I am not loved." But men and women alike can experience attacks against our self-worth in which the liar and tempter can make the most of our psychology to obscure the honest vision of our dignity.

The seven demons being expelled

Our demons can also be the many distractions that lead to a fixation on the "good things of the world" to the point of idolatry, forgetting the One who created all things good. A survey of the human condition is not necessary to know that everyone has a bit of naughtiness or selfishness in them, as well as battle scars from life's journey. We are all in need of healing and transformation to some degree, and in an ongoing way. Even those who have progressed in their depth of union with Jesus know that coming face to face with the pure love of Jesus sheds light on the interior. There is always room to grow closer to Jesus and cast out those demons, vices, or selfishness that lurk within. For whatever reason Mary Magdalene had those demons, they speak of a need for liberation that is not possible by human strength alone, but requires the power of God. For whatever reason we may have "demons" of our own, we are in need of help. We are in need of a deeper purification. We long for new beginnings. Mary Magdalene likely longed for a new beginning. And then she fixed her gaze on Jesus.

### THE POWER OF PURE & UNCONDITIONAL LOVE: EXPERIENCE OF DIGNITY

Mary felt Jesus' gaze so differently from the way others looked at her. In the mosaic, Jesus stands next to a palm tree, which in Psalm 91/92 stands for the righteous one. His righteousness allows him to look upon her with a pure heart. Mary experiences this. She does not feel like an object for another man's

The gaze between Mary and Jesus

pleasure valued merely for what she can do for others or accomplish in the eyes of the world. Jesus looks at her and sees the beauty of her dignity since she is made in God's image. Yet that image is distorted. She feels enslaved.

Nonetheless, receiving his gaze of love constitutes a powerful and decisive moment. She becomes an icon of hope for future generations. No matter her past, present, or future, there is an unshakeable truth. There is something within her that can never change. The mere fact that she is created by a loving God gives her a tremendous value. Her worth in Jesus' heart did not disappear at the sight of seven demons. Rather, her inherent dignity remains as an echo or silent testimony of her great calling from

The palm tree

which she now feels so far. But that gentle experience of acceptance was enough to encourage her to take the next step: to acknowledge the truth of herself and her need for Jesus. Humility kicks in. A spark of faith and trust ignites and she stretches out her hand to receive the gift.

## THE GIFT OF RECEPTIVITY & FREEDOM

Mary's outstretched hand symbolizes the nature of women and the dynamic of faith: both have an element of receptivity. Women are naturally receptive. Physically, she is the one who receives the man in the conjugal act. Psychologically and emotionally, she is the one who opens wide an empathetic heart and embrace of hospitality. The dynamic of faith also requires receptivity. Faith is God's gift. It is never imposed but, rather, received as a gift. It is an invitation that requires the human response of welcoming. In this sense, God respects each person's freedom. When Jesus stands before Mary Magdalene, she has a tremendous opportunity before her: the potential of greater freedom. She can step beyond a distorted use of free will in which she sought to "liberate herself" from God and his ways, and into a new freedom for giving of herself in a unique and selfless way.

The formation of our freedom is a process that takes place through life's circumstances, convictions that begin to form, and the decisive choices intentionally made. It is a process that requires a human and divine dialogue. Maturing in freedom involves guidance from above and here on earth. In the mosaic, Mary's face is indicative of the starting point of that formation. She looks to Jesus. The constant search for deeper knowledge and intimacy with the Lord is a wise use of personal freedom. Ultimately, the goal is to allow God to work in and through us as he so desires. In the words of Mother Teresa, we need to "give God permission."

During Jesus' public life and in the early formation of the Church, Mary was surrounded by men and women who were learning how to "give God permission." One of the persons who most likely offered guidance was Jesus' mother. Whether by word or example, she was a teacher in the school of freedom and love. We can imagine the women chatting about their discoveries and difficulties, buoying each other up in faith, and reminding each other of Jesus' teachings. The men also likely asked Jesus' mother to share with them her own challenges. How many undocumented conversations took place! But a few took root in the heart of the evangelists and were retold.

Mary, the Mother of Jesus, gives us her example with her fiat: "Behold the handmaid of the Lord. Let it be done to me according to your word" (Luke 1:38). Her use of freedom, in obedience, bore life-giving fruit for the salvation of all. Through her surrendering and trusting cooperation with the Holy Spirit, she ushered in the Savior of the world. Surely this was a moment for which God prepared her, assisting her with his grace to become a vessel for the Son of God. But it still required her total acceptance and cooperation with a plan that even she did not understand.

Mary Magdalene's situation was quite different from the mother of Jesus, yet the dynamics are similar. God the Father had his eyes on Mary Magdalene and likely prepared the moment of the encounter between her and his Son. He knew her past, present, and future. He knew how life circumstances influenced some of those choices. He knew the free choices she would make. And he offered her His grace as well as human guidance along the path she would choose.

## THE JOURNEY CONTINUES: THE SCHOOL OF FREEDOM & LOVE

The mosaic portrays the moment when Mary Magdalene stands at a crossroad. She has a choice between an old way of life and a new beginning. Her new beginning is precisely that: a beginning. It is not definitive. The same holds true in our own life. Some people experience marked moments of a "before" and "after" conversion. Others experience the gentle prodding of the Lord many times throughout their life. In either case, God continually invites us to keep walking forward.

Mary's feet

In the mosaic, one of Mary Magdalene's feet is standing solidly upon the rock, while the other is slightly in motion. Her conviction and determination to begin a new life help her to remain "rooted" for what is to come. But she must walk forward from that moment. Her love must mature. She takes a step towards Jesus, who is not only her life but now also her way. The redemption won by Jesus, and applied through the free acceptance in faith, offers a New Way, that is forged day by day, but not without help.

Going back to Jesus' words about the finger of God brings to mind the second passage of Exodus. God's pedagogy and loving providence, depicted by his "finger," become evident. It reads, "When the Lord finished speaking to Moses on Mount Sinai, he gave him the two tablets of the covenant law, the tablets of stone inscribed by the finger of God" (Exodus 31:18). Moses came down from Mount Sinai with the two tablets only to discover that the people had already gotten side-tracked and were worshipping a golden calf. God constantly guided his people with indications, commands, encouragement, and raising up of leaders to assist the journey. His pedagogy is to offer "guidelines." But once again, human freedom comes into play. His way can be accepted or rejected on a daily basis. With the coming of Jesus, a New Covenant is offered to aid the journey towards true liberation. Jesus, through his Holy Spirit, offers a New Law. Jesus is the *New Law*. He is the *Way*.

Mary, being a bold and independent woman, must have desired to be free to forge her path. She had to learn which path led to false freedom and which to true freedom. Along the journey, she continued to experience her weaknesses and sinfulness. After her conversion, she may have questioned if she truly had freedom. She was still beset with temptations. She had to deal with the same cultural problems and challenges. People still treated her the same way and she had no control over that. And Jesus was sometimes demanding in his teachings.

Perhaps she asked the questions that so many ask today: Does all of this predetermine who I will become? What sort of freedom do I really have? It seems that there are situations out of my power that constantly condition my freedom: the culture and religion of birth, the formation received, treatment for good or for worse, self-perceptions, temperament, and the spiritual influences both internal and external that plague or help a person. While freedom appears to be conditioned by so many factors, God sees the big picture and can work all things for the good of those who love him (Romans 8:28).

We all possess intrinsic freedom by the mere fact of being human. But the liberating exercise of our free will takes place in the moral and spiritual realm when we live according to our identity, no matter the external circumstances or "conditions." Jesus says, "The truth will set you free" (Jn. 8:32). Through the exercise of our God-given free will, in response to God's love, we come to a greater participation in the life of Christ. Jesus taught us that true freedom consists of sacrificial love through obedience to God. In John 10:18 he says, "No one can take my life from me. I sacrifice it voluntarily. For I have the authority to lay it down when I want to and also to take it up again. For this is what my Father has commanded." Mary Magdalene was a first-hand witness. Her freedom matured at the foot of the cross, seeing his ultimate sacrifice freely chosen out of love. And she learnt from Mary, his mother, as they stood side by side. They both freely chose to remain, rather than flee in fear or discomfort.

Mary Magdalene's free choice to follow Jesus will bear fruit in an ever greater freedom. The mosaic portrays her rose-colored top, symbolizing the new life she has received. The Kingdom of God has come upon her. In contrast, the ragged skirt symbolizes the life she is leaving behind. While she is made new, she remains Mary Magdalene. Her past is a part of who she is, but now it can be re-integrated into her life project in light of being redeemed. As a new creature in God's Kingdom, she is armed with faith, trust, and love. But since it is unfamiliar territory for her, she may stumble and fall every once in a while. Her heart will continue to be purified as she learns what this way of loving entails. Her newfound faith and trust will be tested to forge all the human elements in fire, strengthening those "spiritual muscles" that were weak from lack of use or a disorderly use. Mary Magdalene will continue her journey through the Galilee with Jesus and his band, to the cross, to confusion at the empty tomb, to excitement at his resurrection, and to trials and triumphs in the early Church. Each day her freedom will be tested, and with it, her love for Jesus will grow. Her journey teaches us a timeless lesson: Our freedom needs to be educated, formed, checked, and used towards the ultimate freedom that can be attained here on earth – to love with the sentiments and heart of Jesus, as Mary learned to do.

Mary Magdalene, rosy top and raggedy skirt

# CONCLUSION

After two thousand years of reflection, we are still gleaning treasures from Mary Magdalene. She is a mystery, in the sense that we know so little about the particularities of her person and life. But at the same time, her "mystery" is unveiled through manifold interpretations and reflections through history. We know enough to see a woman who stands at the center of the greatest events in history, the mystery of God's love for each one of us. She experienced it within. And she continues to announce it today. Pope Benedict XVI sums it up in his audience from July 23, 2006.

> The story of Mary Magdalene reminds everyone of a fundamental truth: She is a disciple of Christ who, in the experience of human weakness, has had the humility to ask for his help, has been healed by him, and has followed him closely, becoming a witness of the power of his merciful love, which is stronger than sin and death.[98]

Mary Magdalene proves to us that the journey of a true disciple is one of freedom and love; and it is possible. Having learned from her, and the multitude of saints in God's family, it is now our turn to discover the unconditional love of God and the dignity we possess. From that starting point, may it strengthen us in faith and hope when we come to the foot of the cross with Jesus. Looking beyond the cross, may we touch the resurrected Christ and be immersed in the love of the Spirit, so we too may go forth and proclaim the Good News: Jesus has truly risen! He is alive! Amen! Alleluia!

## PRAYER TO THE LORD,
## ECHOING THE SENTIMENTS OF MARY MAGDALENE

Lord Jesus, transform my heart with your personal and unconditional love. Heal my brokenness, restore my dignity, and cast out all that prevents a deeper relationship with you. Through the gift of Redemption, may I experience authentic freedom. Grant me fortitude so that I may faithfully follow you, even in the shadow of the Cross. Pour out your Spirit upon me that I may passionately witness to the Good News of your victory over sin and death. And at the end of this earthly pilgrimage, may I be with you forever in your Kingdom. Amen.

# APPENDIX

## Comparative Chart of the Anointing of Jesus

Three passages tell the story of a woman who anoints Jesus. The chart below compares the details of the three passages.

| | LUKE 7:36-50 | JOHN 12:1-8 | MATTHEW 26:6-13 |
|---|---|---|---|
| When? | During Jesus' public ministry | Before Passover (6 days) | Before Passover (at least 2 days) |
| Where? | Possibly the Galilee area | Bethany | Bethany |
| Whose house? | Simon the *Pharisee's* house | Unknown, but Lazarus is at table. | Simon the *Leper's* house |
| Which woman? | "A woman in that town who lived a sinful life" | Mary of Bethany, Martha's and Lazarus' sister | "a woman" |
| Ointment and container? | Alabaster jar with ointment | Pure nard | Alabaster jar with ointment |
| Her actions? | Cleaned his feet with her tears and hair<br><br>She kisses his feet<br><br>Anointed his feet with ointment | Anointed Jesus' feet with ointment<br><br>Wiped Jesus' feet with her hair | Pours the ointment on his head |
| Jesus' words? | "Your sins are forgiven." (because of her great love)<br><br>"Your faith has saved you. Go in peace." | "Let her keep it for my burial."<br><br>"The poor are with you always…" | "She has prepared me for burial."<br><br>"Poor are with you always…"<br><br>"What she has done will be told in remembrance of her." |

# BIBLIOGRAPHY & SUGGESTED RESOURCES FOR FURTHER READING AND RESEARCH

*Where possible, I have provided the website addresses for your further reading or research.*

Aviam, Mordechai. **The Decorated Stone from the Synagogue at Migdal**, A Holistic Interpratation and a Glimpse into the Life of Galilean Jews at the Time of Jesus. Novum Testamentum 55 (2013) 205-220.

Avshalom Gorni, Dina and Arfan Najjar. **Migdal**. Hadashot Archeologyot 125 (2013), http://www.hadashot-esi.org.il/report_detail_eng.aspx?id=2304 (last accessed March 2018).

Avshalom-Gorni, Dina and Edna J. Stern. **Migdal Final Report 30/08/2016**. Hadashot Arkheologiyot: Excavations and Surveys in Israel, Volume 128 (2016). http://www.hadashot-esi.org.il/report_detail_eng.aspx?id=25051&mag_id=124, (accessed February 2018).

Bartunek, Fr John. https://www.spiritualdirection.com/2017/11/16/differences-in-demon-possession-mental-ilness-or-depression, (accessed February 2018).

Bauckham, Richard. **Further Thoughts on the Migdal Synagogue Stone**. Novum Testamentum, Volume 57, Issue 2, pages 113 – 135.

Bauckham, Richard and Stefano De Luca. **"Magdala as we now know it."** Early Christianity 6 (2015); 91-118.

Ben Zion, Ilan. **2,200-year-old bronze artifacts found at biblical site**. Times of Israel, April 5, 2016. https://www.timesofisrael.com/2200-year-old-bronze-artifacts-found-at-biblical-site/. (Last accessed February 2018).

Binder, Donald D. **The Mystery of the Magdala Stone** in Daniel A. Warner and Donald D. Binder, ed., *A City Set on a Hill: Essays in Honor of James F. Strange* (Mountain Home: Border Stone Press, 2014), 17-48.

Borschel-Dan, Amanda. **New finds suggest Second Temple priests who fled the Romans kept up holy rituals in the Galilee**. *Times of Israel*, July 26, 2017. https://www.timesofisrael.com/new-finds-suggest-second-temple-priests-who-fled-the-romans-kept-up-holy-rituals-in-the-galilee/ (Last accessed February 2018).

Bovon, Francois. **Luke 1: A Commentary on the Gospel of Luke 1:1-9:50**. Hermeneia 63A; ed. Helmut Koester; trans. Christine M. Thomas; Accordance electronic ed. (Minneapolis: Fortress Press, 2002), 301.

Bruckberger, Raymond L, OP. **Maria Magdalena**. Edited by Jack Tollers, Smashwords Edition, (January 2014).

Canonical Gospel texts: (New International Version), https://www.biblegateway.com/ (Last accessed June 2018).

Carpenter, Chris. **The Truth Behind the DaVinci Code, CBN.com interview,** http://www1.cbn.com/books/the-truth-behind-the-davinci-code, (Accessed February 2018).

Chancey, Mark. **Greco-Roman Culture and the Galilee of Jesus**. *Society for New Testament Studies Monograph Series*, 134. Cambridge: Cambridge University Press, (2006). pp 304.

Chancey, Mark. **The Myth of the Galilee Gentile**. Cambridge University Press; 1 edition, (May 23, 2002).

Christian Classics Ethereal Library, Golden Legend. Volume 4, Of Mary Magdalene, http://www.ccel.org/ccel/voragine/goldleg4.xv.html?highlight=mary,magdalene#highlight (accessed January 2018).

Cinamon, Gilad. **Migdal: Final Report** (16 Sep 2014). *Hadashot Arkheologiyot* 126 (2014). http://www.hadashot-esi.org.il/report_detail_eng.aspx?id=11620&mag_id=121. (Last accessed February 2018).

Corbo, Virgilio. **La Città Romana di Magdala: Rapporto Preliminare dopo la Quarta Campagna di Scavo: 1 Ottobre – 8 Dicembre 1975**. Pp. 355-378 in E. Testa, I. Mancini and M. Piccirillo ed., Studia Hierosolymitana in Onore di P. Bellarmino Bagatti, vol. 1: Studi Archeologici (SBF Collectio Maior 22; Jerusalem: Franciscan Printing Press, 1976).

Corbo, Virgilio. **Scavi Archeologici a Magdala** (1971-1973). *Liber Annuus* 24 (1974) 5-37.

Corbo, Virgilio. **La Piazza e Villa Urbana a Magdala**. *Liber Annuus* 28 (1978), 232-240.

Davidson, Fr Sean. **Mary Magdalene: Prophetess of Eucharistic Love**. Ignatius Press, (Jan 2017).

Ehrman, Bart. **Peter, Paul & Mary Magdalene: The Followers of Jesus in History and Legend**. New York: Oxford Press, (2006), pp 211-213.

El Proyecto Arqueológico Magdala. **Interpretaciones preliminares bajo una** perspectiva interdisciplinar. *El Pensador*, Numero 5, Año 1, (Oct 2013).

Fitzmyer, Joseph. The Gospel According to Luke I-IX, The Anchor Yale Bible. (New Haven: Yale University Press, 1974), 697-698.

Hachlili, Rachel. **Synagogues: Before and After the Roman Destruction of the Temple**. Biblical Archaeology Review 41. 3 (May/Jun 2015): 30–38, 65.

Hesemann, Michael. **Mary Magdalene in History, Tradition and Legend**. (2013). http://michaelhesemann.info/10_3.html#_ftnref58 (Last accessed March 2018).

Josephus, Flavius. **War of the Jews**, Book 3, Chapter 10, & **The Life of Flavius Josephus**, 141-142. http://www.sacred-texts.com/jud/josephus/. (Last accessed March 2018).

Kershner, Isabel. **A Carved Stone Block Upends Assumptions About Ancient Judaism**. (*New York Times*, Dec 8, 2015). https://www.nytimes.com/2015/12/09/world/middleeast/magdala-stone-israel-judaism.html?mwrsm=Email&_r=0#story-continues-1

Lawlor, Paula. **Mary Magdalene in the South of France**. California: Magdalene Publishing. 2012, p3.

Lena, Anna. **Magdala 2008 Preliminary Report**. *Hadashot Arkheologiyot*: Excavations and Surveys in Israel, Volume 125 Year 2013, 31/12/2013 http://www.hadashot-esi.org.il/report_detail_eng.aspx?id=5433 (accessed February 2018).

Marcela Zapata-Meza. **The Fishy Secret to Ancient Magdala's Economic Growth: Cornering the Salted Fish Market**. *Biblical Archaeology Review*, 08/09/2016. http://www.biblicalarchaeology.org/daily/biblical-sites-places/biblical-archaeology-places/the-fishy-secret-to-ancient-magdalas-economic-growth (Last accessed January 2018).

**Mary Magdalene, Apostle of the Apostles**. Holy See Press Office, 10.06.2016. https://press.vatican.va/content/salastampa/en/bollettino/pubblico/2016/06/10/160610c.html (accessed January 2018).

McDaniel, Thomas F., Ph.D. **Clarifying Baffling Biblical Passage**. Chapter 32: The Meaning of "Mary", "Magdalene", and other Names, 2002. http://www.google.com/url?sa=t&rct=j&q=&esrc=s&source=web&cd=1&ved=0ahUKEwi24Yrl9ZjZAhUEC8AKHW6KBOIQFggqMAA&url=http%3A%2F%2Ftmcdaniel.palmerseminary.edu%2Fcbbp-book.pdf&usg=AOvVaw2BbNIq9EP74hvQbula7Eex

Mowczko, Marg. **Galilee in the First Century CE**. http://margmowczko. com/galilee-first-century-ce/

Neubauer, Adolphe. **La géographie du Talmud**. (Paris: Michel Lévy Fréres, 1868).

Nollan, John. Luke 1-9:20, WBC35A; Accordance electronic ed. (Grand Rapids: Zondervan, 1989), 366.

Reich, Ronny and Marcela Zapata-Meza. **A Preliminary Report on the Mikwa'ot of Migdal**, *Israel Exploration Journal* 64,1 (2014), 63-71.

Sanidopulous, John. **The Seven Demons of Mary Magdalene**. *Daimonologia*, (July 2015), http://www.daimonologia.org/2015/07/the-seven-demons-of-mary-magdalene.html (accessed February 2018).

Skinner, Andrew. **A Historical Sketch of Galilee**. *BYU Studies Quarterly*, Volume 36, Issue 3, Article 8, (1996). https://scholarsarchive.byu.edu/cgi. (Last accessed February 2018).

Stracke, Richard. **Saint Mary Magdalene: The Iconography**. (2017). http://www.christianiconography.info/magdalene.html .(Last accessed March 2018).

Textual references to Church Fathers (up to 6th century) referring to Mary Magdalene: http://arthistoryresources.net/investigating-mary-magdalen/mm-church-fathers.html (accessed February 2018).

Tohoroth, Seder. **Pools of Immersion**, Chapter 1, Mishnah 8, https://halakhah.com/. (accessed February 2018).

Vamosh, Miriam Feinberg. **Women at the Time of the Bible**. (Israel: Palphot Ltd., 2007).

Various Art works through the centuries on Mary Magdalene can be accessed through https://www.wikiart.org/en/Search/Mary%20Magdalene. (Last accessed March 2018)

Welborn, Amy. **Decoding Mary Magdalene: Truth, Legend, and Lies**. (Indiana: Our Sunday Visitor, 2006).

Wray, Dr TJ. **Good Girls Bad Girls of the New Testament**. (Rowman & Littlefield, 2016).

Website for Canonical & Apocryphal Gospels and Early Church Fathers' writing: http://www.earlychristianwritings.com, (accessed February 2018).

## ENDNOTES

1   Arfan Najjar, IAA excavator from 2009-2017, estimated that Magdala's population in the first century was probably about 4,000 people, making it one of the larger towns on the shores of the Sea of Galilee. This data is still awaiting further confirmation. Magdala has long been associated with the town of Taricheae, the "place of salted fish." Josephus wrote that at one time, 40,000 people were gathered in a hippodrome to accuse him of treason. From the text it appears that he is speaking of the combination of the those living in Magdala and those who gathered from various towns around Magdala-Taricheae. (Josephus. War, Book 2, XXI. 4. http://www.sacred-texts.com/jud/josephus/war-2.htm). Around 1920, William Albright, an American archaeologist, proposed that Taricheae was north of Tiberias. He based himself on Josephus' text that describes Taricheae at the base of a mountain, fitting the geographical area of ancient Magdala. (Josephus, War, Book 3, X, 1. http://www.sacred-texts.com/jud/josephus/war-3.htm). With the discovery of ancient Magdala, the association between Magdala and Taricheae was reinforced. Magdala's identification as Taricheae is currently challenged by Nikos Kokkinos (http://www.magdalaproject.org/WP/?p=3782). He states that Pliny's Natural History, written in 77 CE, locates the town of Taricheae on the south-west shore of the Sea of Galilee.

2   *Antiquity of the Jews*, Book XIV.7.3 , http://www.ccel.org/j/josephus/works/ant-14.htm (accessed Jan 2018)

3   An initial theory proposed the possibility of the town being abandoned due to the killing and enslavement of the inhabitants. Further excavations in the summer of 2017 led to the discovery of pottery remains that revealed reoccupation after 67 AD. A new theory is being considered, that "common life just continued, but not in the same way, until the northern area was finally abandoned during the second century" (Rosaura Sanz, excavator, email conversation, March 2018). If Kokkinos' theory is correct, and Magdala is not Taricheae, then this currently excavated town of Magdala, may not have been so heavily affected by the Great Jewish Revolt.

4   "Christian sources state that in the eighth–tenth centuries CE, under Muslim rule, a church stood at the site identified as the home of Mary Magdalene. During the early days of the Crusader Kingdom of Jerusalem, Abbot Daniel mentions the home of Mary Magdalene in his writings from 1106–1108 CE. (...) In 1283 CE, Burchard of Mount Sion wrote about his visit to the home of Mary Magdalene. Several years later, toward the end of the Crusader kingdom, the Italian monk Riccoldo da Monte di Croce (Ricoldus of Montecroce) arrived in Magdala and burst into tears of joy at the sight of the beautiful church that still stood there. During the Mamluk and Ottoman periods, the village of Magdala was mentioned just once, in 1626 CE; in this source, people claimed to have seen the home of Mary Magdalene, although by then the site was already a ruin (Pringle 1998:28). In the nineteenth century, Guérin and the members of the PEF

survey described the Arab village of Majdal as comprising about thirty houses and eighty inhabitants. The Arab village, which preserved the ancient name as Majdal, was situated within the boundaries of ancient Migdal, and existed until the War of Independence…" Avshalom-Gorni, Dina and Edna J. Stern, Migdal Final Report 30/08/2016. *Hadashot Arkheologiyot*: Excavations and Surveys in Israel, Volume 128 Year 2016. http://www.hadashot-esi.org.il/report_detail_eng.aspx?id=25051&mag_id=124;

5    "On April 24-25, 1935, on instructions from the Custos, Fr. Nazzareno Iacopozzi, Fr. S. Saller and I visited the place to study the ruins, with the help of by Fr. Gregorio Ocio, warden of the Franciscan Hospice in Tiberias. The village muktar Mutlaq, with the many children and grandchildren from his nine wives, sufficient to form a village, showed us all the ruins, visible and invisible, since he expected to sell them to the Custody of the Holy Land. On this occasion we made a rough plan of the antiquities which still has documentary value since no further excavations and surveys have been carried out at the place." http://www.magdalaproject.org/WP/?p=742

6    De Luca, Stefano. *Note per la storia di Magdala*, (2006), http://www.magdalaproject.org/WP/?page_id=70&langswitch_lang=it

7    By Underwood & Underwood, Book author: Robert Smythe Hichens The Holy Land, 1910 p.121, Public Domain, https://commons.wikimedia.org/w/index.php?curid=6755119)

8    See footnote #1.

9    *The Life of Flavius*, 142, http://lexundria.com/j_vit/132-154/wst (accessed Jan 2018), Bradley Root, author of *First Century Galilee: A Fresh Examination of the Sources*, interprets the abundance of people fleeing to the city as likely being Jewish refugees who came to join the Judean revolution.

10   El Proyecto Arqueológico Magdala. *Interpretaciones preliminares bajo una perspectiva interdisciplinar*. El Pensador, Numero 5, Año 1, OCT 2013, p. 9,18.

11   Mark Chancey's 2008 work *Greco-Roman Culture and the Galilee of Jesus* wrote: "Hellenization or Romanization in one aspect of culture should not be automatically interpreted as evidence for Hellenization or Romanization in another aspect of culture. Neither Hellenization nor Romanization should be understood to indicate total replacement of local, indigenous cultures." On the other hand, Bradley Root, author of First Century Galilee: A Fresh Examination of the Sources, is of the opinion that Magdala was likely more Hellenized in comparison to inland settlements in Galilee. In an email conversation, February 2018, he commented that "the recent discoveries by De Luca and Bauckham certainly indicate that the residents of Magdala had somewhat different religious/cultural norms than many other Galileans."

12   Bauckham, Richard and Stefano De Luca: "Magdala as we now know it", *Early Christianity* 6 (2015); 91-118.

13   Two parcels of land have been excavated, uncovering the ancient Magdala. As early as the 1930s the Franciscans were tipped off by local residents about the ruins of ancient Magdala. Excavations began in the early 1970s. In 2006, Fr Juan Solana, LC, began an initiative of building a guest house on the properties to the north of the excavation site. This led to the 2009 discovery of the northern side of ancient Magdala.

14   Bauckham, Richard and Stefano De Luca: "Magdala as we now know it", *Early Christianity* 6 (2015); 91-118.

15   There is a slight difference between the meander mosaics. In the Southern excavation's Bathhouse and the Northern excavation's Synagogue, it is a cross meander with a single turn, alternated with squares. The Northern excavation's Mikva'ot area mosaic does not contain squares (Rosaura Sanz, Northern Magdala excavator, March 2018).

16   The Mikva'ot complex consists of two large complexes with multiple rooms, four purification baths, and the floor with a mosaic. Many refer to this area as an indication of wealth in the town.

17   It is stated as 30 furlongs in The Life of Flavius Josephus, 32, http://www.sacred-texts.com/jud/josephus/autobiog.htm (accessed February 3, 2018)

18   Marcela Zapata-Meza, The Fishy Secret to Ancient Magdala's Economic Growth, Cornering the salted fish market, *Biblical Archaeology Review*, 08/09/2016

19   http://www.hadashot-esi.org.il/Images//6022-14.jpg; courtesy of IAA

20   Avshalom Gorni, Dina and Arfan Najjar, Migdal, *Hadashot Archeologyot* 125 (2013), http://www.hadashot-esi.org.il/report_detail_eng.aspx?id=2304

21   *The Geography of Strabo*, 45, http://penelope.uchicago.edu/Thayer/e/roman/texts/strabo/16b*.html (Accessed January 2018).

22   Neubauer, Adolphe, *La géographie du Talmud*, Paris : Michel Lévy Fréres, 1868. https://archive.org/stream/bub_gb_DlgYKxhNNL8C#page/n263/mode/2up/search/Genesaret

23   "The country also that lies over against this lake hath the same name of *Gennesareth*; its nature is wonderful as well as its beauty; its soil is so fruitful that all sorts of trees can grow upon it, and the inhabitants accordingly plant all sorts of trees there; for the temper of the air is so well mixed that it agrees very well with those several sorts, particularly walnuts, which require the coldest

air, flourish there in vast plenty; there are palm trees also, which grow best in hot air; fig trees also and olives grow near them, which yet require an air that is more temperate. One may call this place the ambition of nature, where it forces those plants that are naturally enemies to one another to agree together: it is a happy contention of the seasons, as if every one of them laid claim to this country; for it not only nourishes different sorts of autumnal fruit beyond men's expectation, but preserves them a great while; it supplies men with the principal fruits, with grapes and figs, continually, during ten months of the year, (11) and the rest of the fruits as they become ripe together through the whole year: for besides the good temperature of the air, it is also watered from a most fertile fountain. The people of the country call it *Capharnaum*. Some have thought it to be a vein of the Nile, because it produces the Coracin fish as well as that lake does which is near to Alexandria. The length of this country extends itself along the banks of this lake that bears the same name for thirty furlongs, and is in breadth twenty, And this is the nature of that place." Flavius Josephus, The War of the Jews, Book 3, chapter 10.8, https://www.ccel.org/ccel/josephus/complete.iii.iv.x.html

24  Lena, Anna. Magdala 2008 Preliminary Report, *Hadashot Arkheologiyot*: Excavations and Surveys in Israel, Volume 125 Year 2013, 31/12/2013 http://www.hadashot-esi.org.il/report_detail_eng.aspx?id=5433

25  *Seder Tohoroth*, Pools of Immersion, Chapter 1, Mishnah 8, https://halakhah.com/

26  Email conversation with Professor Marcela Zapata, December 18, 2017.

27  Avshalom Gorni, Dina and Arfan Najjar, Migdal, *Hadashot Archeologyot* 125 (2013), http://www.hadashot-esi.org.il/report_detail_eng.aspx?id=2304

28  Hachlili, Rachel. "Synagogues: Before and After the Roman Destruction of the Temple." *Biblical Archaeology Review* 41.3 (May/Jun 2015): 30–38, 65.

29  Vamosh, Miriam Feinberg. *Women at the Time of the Bible*, (Israel: Palphot Ltd.), 2007. This source quotes from the Babylonian Talmud, Avoda Zara 38a. The Babylonian Talmud is a collection of thousands of rabbinical teachings compiled between the third to fifth centuries AD. It includes reflections on everything from law, history, worship, philosophy, and more. After the destruction of the Temple 70 AD, the rabbis faced the challenge of a Jerusalem without a Temple and central place of teaching. The dispersion of Jews also motivated the rabbis to begin documenting legal aspects and commentaries for righteous living for future generations. The specific tract called the Avoda Zara was written in response to threats of idolatry. The Jewish people often experienced the threat of assimilating pagan cultic elements into their own. Idolatry was the gravest sin and often identified with immoral conduct, such as seen in fertility cults. It was equivalent to rejecting the entire Torah. https://halakhah.com/zarah/index.html#intro

30   Vamosh, Miriam Feinberg. *Women at the Time of the Bible*, (Israel: Palphot Ltd.), 2007. This source quotes from the Talmudic Tractate Megilla 23a.

31   Magdala Visitors' Statistics recorded between March 2014 and April 2018

32   Fine, Steven, From Synagogue Furnishing to Media Event: The Magdala Ashlar, *Arts Judaica*, 2017, pp 27-38.

33   Aviam, Mordechai. The Decorated Stone from the Synagogue at Migdal, A Holistic Interpratation and a Glimpse into the Life of Galilean Jews at the Time of Jesus. *Novum Testamentum* 55 (2013) 205-220.

34   Isabel Kershner, "A Carved Stone Block Upends Assumptions About Ancient Judaism," (New York Times, Dec 8, 2015). https://www.nytimes.com/2015/12/09/world/middleeast/magdala-stone-israel-judaism.html?mwrsm=Email&_r=0#story-continues-1

35   Bauckham, Richard, Further Thoughts on the Migdal Synagogue Stone, *Novum Testamentum*, Volume 57, Issue 2, pages 113 – 135.

36   A replica of the Menorah carving in the priests' mansion can be seen in the Wohl museum in the Jewish quarter of the Old City of Jerusalem.

37   Image licensed under the Creative Commons Attribution 3.0 unported. Title: Roman Triumphal arch panel copy from Beth Hatefuthsoth, showing the spoils of Jerusalem Temple. Original file by Steerpike. This image has been cut from the original to focus only on the menorah. Accessed May 1, 2018, https://upload.wikimedia.org/wikipedia/commons/0/05/Arch_of_Titus_Menorah_22.jpg

38   This video may be accessed through https://www.youtube.com/watch?v=cWO8WJ6oOZU (posted in February 2016, accessed in March 2018).

39   Ratzinger, Joseph. *Jesus of Nazareth, Part Two*. San Francisco: Ignatius Press. 2011, pp. 25-26.

40   Cohen, Shaye. *"The Significance of Yavneh and Other Essays in Jewish Hellenism."* Mohr Siebeck, 2010., p. 32.

41   Goldman, Talia. *Prostitution in Classical and Jewish Antiquity*. Hashta: Jewish Voices on a Secular Campus. https://sites.google.com/site/hashtaumd/contents-1/prost (accessed April 20, 2018).

42   Josephus, Flavius, *War of the Jews*, Book 3, Chapter 10. http://www.sacred-texts.com/jud/josephus/war-3.htm (accessed April 16, 2018). Flavius is often accused of exaggerating numbers, however his description gives the sense of the enormity and brutality of the event.

43  https://www.christianitytoday.com/news/2018/january/top-50-christian-persecution-open-doors-world-watch-list.html

44  "On April 24-25, 1935, on instructions from the Custos, Fr. Nazzareno Iacopozzi, Fr. S. Saller and I visited the place to study the ruins, with the help of by Fr. Gregorio Ocio, warden of the Franciscan Hospice in Tiberias. The village muktar Mutlaq, with the many children and grandchildren from his nine wives, sufficient to form a village, showed us all the ruins, visible and invisible, since he expected to sell them to the Custody of the Holy Land. On this occasion we made a rough plan of the antiquities which still has documentary value since no further excavations and surveys have been carried out at the place." http://www.magdalaproject.org/WP/?p=742

45  References with Mary Magdalene's full name: Mt 27:55, 27:61, 28:1; Mk 15:40, 15:47, 16:1; Lk 8:2, 24:10; Jn 19:25, 20:1, 20:18

46  Considering the number of ossuaries with inscribed names, Michael Hesemann suggests that ¼ of female in that period were named with a variation of Mary. Accessed March 2018 from Mary Magdalene in History, Tradition and Legend, http://michaelhesemann.info/10_3.html#_ftnref58.

47  The following examples are expounded upon in McDaniel, Thomas F., Ph.D. *Clarifying Baffling Biblical Passage*, Chapter 32 the Meaning of "Mary", "Magdalene", and other names, 2002.

48  Sanidopulous, John. The Seven Demons of Mary Magdalene. *Daimonolgia*, July 2015, http://www.daimonologia.org/2015/07/the-seven-demons-of-mary-magdalene.html

49  Wray, Dr TJ. *Good Girls Bad Girls of the New Testament*. (Rowman & Littlefield, 2016), p. 79.

50  Fitzmyer, Joseph. *The Gospel According to Luke I-IX*, The Anchor Yale Bible; (New Haven: Yale University Press, 1974), 697-698.

    Nollan, John, *Luke 1-9:20*, WBC35A; Accordance electronic ed. (Grand Rapids: Zondervan, 1989), 366.

    Bovon, Francois, *Luke 1: A Commentary on the Gosepl of Luke 1:1-9:50*, Hermeneia 63A; ed. Helmut Koester; trans. Christine M. Thomas; Accordance electronic ed. (Minneapolis: Fortress Press, 2002), 301.

51  https://www.spiritualdirection.com/2017/11/16/differences-in-demon-possession-mental-illness-or-depression; Fr Bartunek discusses the open door created by dabbling in the occult, New Age and Wiccan practices.

52  For more information on this subject: Amorth, Gabriele, *An Exorcist Tells His Story*. Ignatius Press, 1999.

53  Denisse Bossert is a syndicated U.S. diocesan columnist, author, and speaker. She is author of Stations of the Cross for a Wounded World. She is a victim of sexual abuse and rape and shares her story of healing. https://www.youtube.com/watch?v=5FZIWrFGT3k; https://www.facebook.com/denise.bossert/posts/1831163883770794

54  According to the Talmudic tract, *Semahot*, women were allowed to prepare the bodies of men for burial.

55  For more information on the Shroud of Turin: http://www.shroudofturin.com/; http://www.shroud.com/. The original Shroud of Turin is stored in Turin, Italy. Museums displaying replicas exist in The Turin Shroud Center of Colorado http://www.shroudofturin.com/exhibit.html; The Shrine of the Most Blessed Sacrament http://www.olamshrine.com/sites/shroud-of-turin-and-lower-church/;, and Notre Dame of Jerusalem https://www.notredamecenter.org/shroud-exhibition. A. Danin, Botany of the Shroud of Turin: The Story of Floral Images on the Shroud of Turin, Jerusalem: Danin Publishing, 2010.

56  https://www.catholicculture.org/culture/liturgicalyear/activities/view.cfm?id=1044

57  Amy Welborn, *Decoding Mary Magdalene: Truth, Legend, and Lies*. (Indiana: Our Sunday Visitor, 2006); For quick online reference to this theme see Chris Carpenter's, The Truth Behind the DaVinci Code, CBN.com interview, http://www1.cbn.com/books/the-truth-behind-the-davinci-code

58  For a further analysis of this modern day movement, read Placuit Deo, *On Certain Aspects of Christian Salvation*,by the Congregation for the Doctrine of the Faith.

59  For further analyses see http://frcoulter.com/presentations/marymagdalene.html; http://www.frcoulter.com/presentations/davincitalk.html;

60  Ehrman, Bart. *Peter, Paul & Mary Magdalene: The Followers of Jesus in History and Legend*. New York: Oxford Press, 2006, pp 211-213.

61  McDaniel, Thomas F., Ph.D. *Clarifying Baffling Biblical Passage*, Chapter 32: The Meaning of "Mary", "Magdalene", and other names, 2002.

62  Church Fathers are defined by the Catholic Church, as such, due to their early Church leadership, doctrinal and theological reflections contributing to the early formation of doctrine, personal sanctity, and living within the first eight centuries of Christianity.

63  St. Gregory of Nyssa, *Against Eunomius*, Book 12. http://www.newadvent.org/fathers/290112.htm

64   St Jerome, Letter 127, http://www.newadvent.org/fathers/3001127.htm

65   St. Augustine, a fourth-century Church Father⊠ echoes the same sentiments as Ephrem. He wrote on the significance of being a bearer of God's truth, but highlighting Mary, the Mother of Jesus. In his Sermon 25 he wrote, "Mary (the Mother of God) heard God's word and kept it, and so she is blessed. She kept God's truth in her mind, a nobler thing than carrying his body in her womb. The truth and the body were both Christ: he was kept in Mary's mind insofar as he is truth, he was carried in her womb insofar as he is man; but what is kept in the mind is of a higher order than what is carried in the womb" https://www.crossroadsinitiative.com/media/articles/thevirginmaryconceivedinfaith/, (accessed March 2018).

66   St Gregory the Great, Book VII, Letter 25, http://www.newadvent.org/fathers/360207025.htm

67   St Gregory the Great, Homily 25, http://www.ibreviary.com/m2/breviario.php?s=ufficio_delle_letture

68   The term "feminine genius" is a concept developed by Edith Stein and promulgated by Pope John Paul II. Our "genius" is God's image in us. And women possess a specifically "feminine genius." For further reflection see, Pope John Paul II, *Letter to Women*. #12, June 29, 1995 (https://w2.vatican.va/content/john-paul-ii/en/letters/1995/documents/hf_jp-ii_let_29061995_women.html).

69   Davidson, Fr Sean. *Mary Magdalene: Prophetess of Eucharistic Love*. Ignatius Press, Jan 2017.

70   Mary Magdalene, apostle of the apostles, Holy See Press Office, 10.06.2016. https://press.vatican.va/content/salastampa/en/bollettino/pubblico/2016/06/10/160610c.html

71   *Ibid.*

72   Matthew 26:6-13 is similar to John 12:1-8; however, Matthew names the house as Simon the Leper's.

73   *The Gospel of Nicodemus*, Chapter 11, http://www.ccel.org/ccel/schaff/anf08.vii.xiii.xii.html?highlight=magdalene#highlight

74   Tacitus, *The Annals*, Book 4, paragraph 67. http://classics.mit.edu/Tacitus/annals.mb.txt

75   Flavius Josephus, *Jewish Antiquities* 18.85-89.

76   https://oca.org/saints/lives/2014/07/22/102070-myrrhbearer-and-equal-of-the-apostles-mary-magdalene

77   © By the Hand of Nicholas P. Papas, npstudiogbg@gmail.com.

78   Christian Classics Ethereal Library, Golden Legend, Volume 4, *Of Mary Magdalene*, http://www.ccel.org/ccel/voragine/goldleg4.xv.html?highlight=mary,magdalene#highlight

79   Hegesippus was a Jewish convert to Christianity, who often was called the Father of Church History. He was born in Jerusalem, and spent several years in Rome, writing his notes on the history of the early Church between 165 and 175.

80   Lawlor, Paula. *Mary Magdalene in the South of France*. California: Magdalene Publishing. 2012, p3.

81   *The Life of our Holy Mother Mary of Egypt*, (From The Great Canon, the Work of Saint Andrew of Crete, Holy Trinity Monastery, Jordanville, NY, USA), http://www.ocf.org/OrthodoxPage/reading/st.mary.html

82   Fresco in the Magdalene Chapel, Basilica of St. Francis, Assisi, 1320s by Giotto http://www.christianiconography.info/Wikimedia%20Commons/magdaleneZosimusGiotto.html (public domain)

83   Catechism of the Catholic Church #1988, http://www.vatican.va/archive/ccc_css/archive/catechism/p3s1c3a2.htm (accessed April 2018)

84   This echoes Saint Irenaeus, "The Glory of God is man fully alive."

85   http://www.christianiconography.info/iconographySupplementalImages/crucifixion/rabbula.html

86   http://www.christianiconography.info/magdalene.html

87   https://www.wikiart.org/en/Search/Fra%20Angelico,%20Mary%20Magdalene; (public domain)

88   https://www.wikiart.org/en/titian/penitent-st-mary-magdalene (public domain)

89   https://www.wikiart.org/en/el-greco/mary-magdalene-in-penitence; (public domain)

90   https://www.wikiart.org/en/Search/Reni,%20Mary%20Magdalene (public domain)

91   https://www.wikiart.org/en/Search/George%20de%20La%20tour (public domain)

92   https://www.wikiart.org/en/el-greco/st-mary-magdalene; (public domain)

93 https://www.wga.hu/art/c/canova/1/5magdale.jpg (public domain)

94 © John Collier, www.Hillstream.com (permission granted)

95 Kanaph is the original Hebrew word used for wings, which means corners. https://www.biblestudytools.com/lexicons/hebrew/nas/kanaph-2.html

96 *Fight the New Drug"* website reports on current facts related to pornography and the harmful effects on our culture. https://fightthenewdrug.org/10-porn-stats-that-will-blow-your-mind/

97 For more information on statistics on sexual assualt and harrassment, see https://www.rainn.org/statistics/victims-sexual-violence

98 Pope Benedict XVI, ANGELUS, Les Combes, 23 July 2006. http://w2.vatican.va/content/benedict-xvi/en/angelus/2006/documents/hf_ben-xvi_ang_20060723.html (accessed March 2018).

Carlos and Rachel Ramirez found treasures in the ground and in each other!
(2011-12 Volunteers; August 1, 2015 – Married in Magdala; 2015–2018 Magdala's Volunteer Coordinators

Printed in Great Britain
by Amazon

57802161R00097